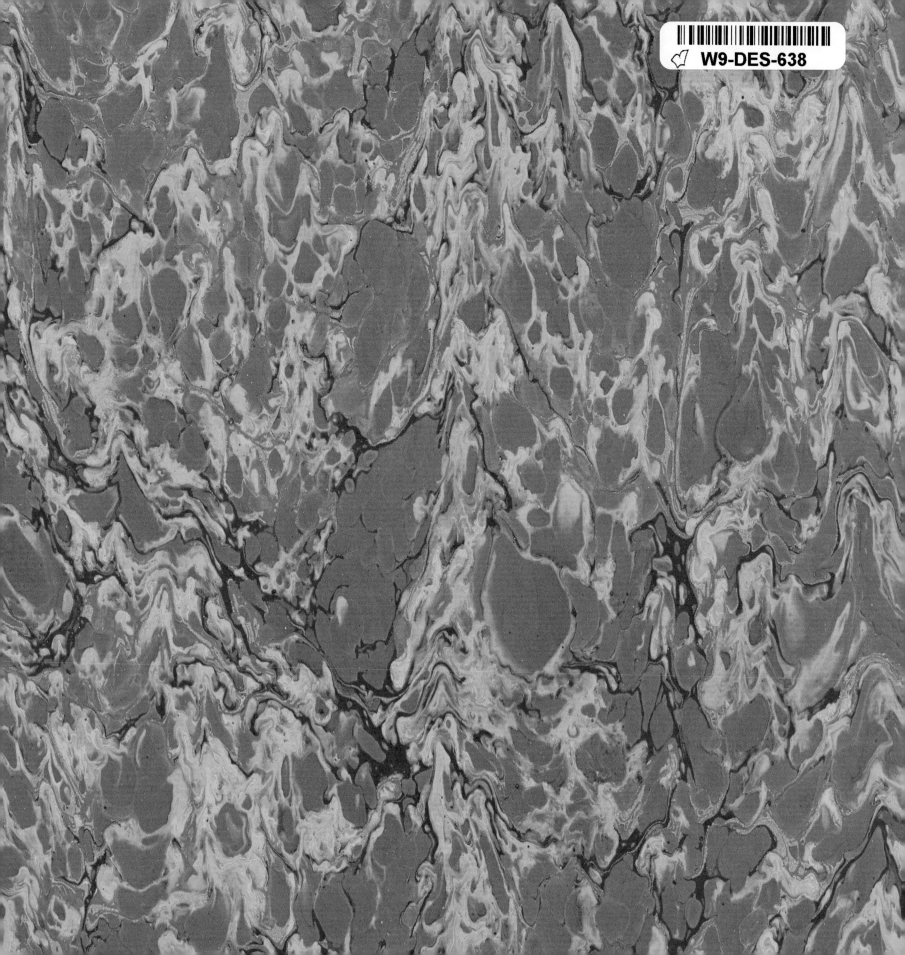

TROMPE L'OEIL AT HOME

TROMPE L'OEIL AT HOME

FAUX FINISHES AND FANTASY SETTINGS

KAREN S. CHAMBERS

FOREWORD BY JOCASTA INNES

RIZZOLI
NEW YORK

First published in the United States of America by

Rizzoli International Publications, Inc.
300 Park Avenue South
New York, NY 10010

The photograph on page 14 courtesy of Zuber & Cie manufacture de papiers peints

TROMPE L'OEIL AT HOME
was conceived and produced by
Running Heads Incorporated
55 West 21 Street
New York, NY 10010

Designer: Liz Trovato
Photo Research: Michelle Hauser and Ellie Watson
Production Manager: Linda Winters

Typeset by Trufont Typographers
Color separations by Hong Kong Scanner Craft Co., Ltd.
Printed and bound in Hong Kong by C&C Offset Printing Co. Ltd.

Library of Congress Cataloging in Publication Data

Chambers, Karen S.
Trompe l'oeil at home : faux finishes and fantasy settings / Karen
S. Chambers.
p.   cm.
Includes bibliographical references and index.
ISBN 0-8478-1420-3
1. Visual perception.   2. Trompe l'oeil painting.   3. Optical
illusions.   4. Illusion in art.   5. Interior decoration.   I. Title.
N7430.5.C48   1991
751.7'3—dc20   91-52799
                                                                CIP

1 3 5 7 9 0 8 6 4 2

For Thalia, I hope she finds it amusing.

ACKNOWLEDGMENTS

Trompe l'Oeil at Home simply would not exist without the very concrete contributions of a number of people. I am indebted to Barbara Flanagan for her thoughts on this subject. At Running Heads I wish to thank Marta Hallett for her encouragement to pursue this mercurial subject, Ellen Milionis for making this book a reality, Mary Forsell and Charles de Kay for their editorial expertise, Michelle Hauser and Ellie Watson for materializing illusionism through their photographic research, Liz Trovato for realizing our illusionistic vision with her wonderful design, Lindsey Crittenden for keeping the project on track, and Linda Winters for her care in making the book as beautiful as it could be.

I would like to acknowledge the assistance of Judy Straeten of Brunschwig & Fils, Alina Slonim of Richard Haas's studio, Dr. Alice Zrebiec, and all the librarians of the New York Public Library who helped me navigate the constantly shifting waters of this topic.

To Lois Baker, Laurinda Dixon, Judith Dupré, Max Harding, Ron Havern, Juliana Hoover, Barbara Mayer, Ruth Meyer, Ken Nichols, and Margaret Richardson, go my thanks for listening to my endless ramblings on this subject. They all helped me to clarify my thoughts.

Karen S. Chambers
New York
January 1990

CONTENTS

III
INSPIRATION
AND APPLICATION 145

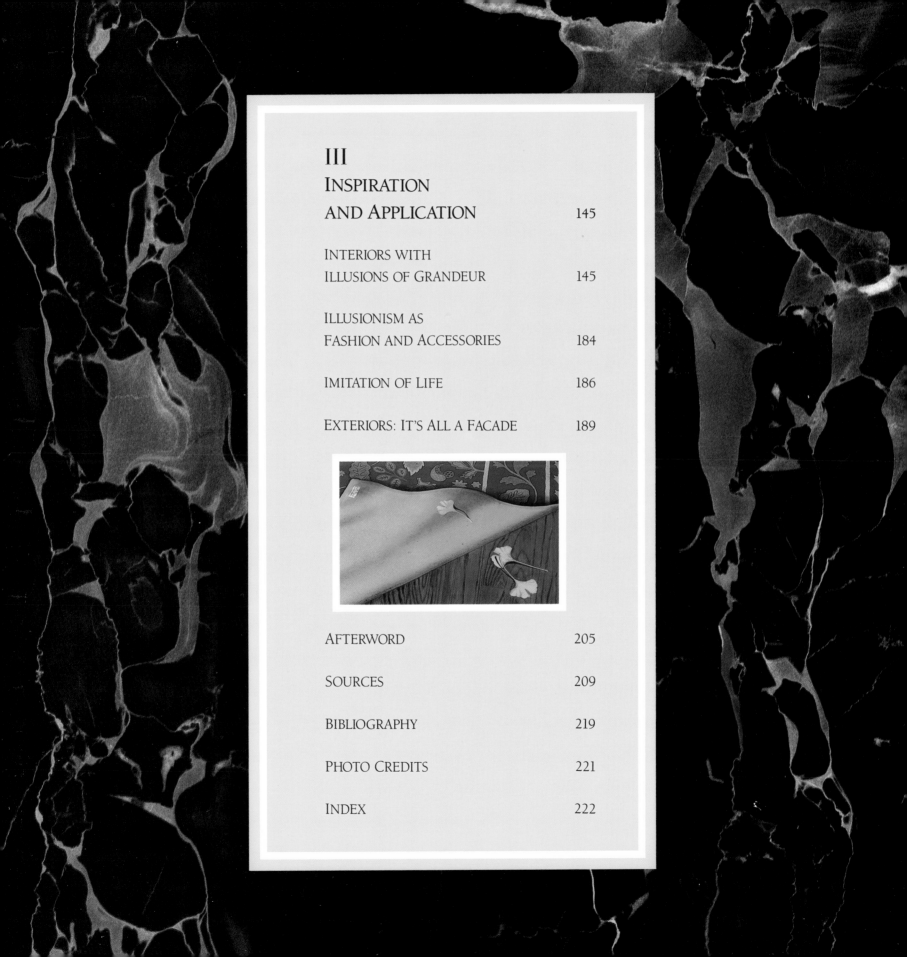

FOREWORD

"Remember that a picture, before being a battle horse, a nude woman, or some anecdote, is essentially a plane surface covered with paint in a certain arrangement." Thus Maurice Denis advised the Nabis painters. His words also act as a reminder to us that visual deception enters into the very act of representing reality on canvas. However realistic the representation, even as meticulous as in the work of Dutch flower painters like Bosschaert, it is not necessarily trompe l'oeil. The eye perceives the distinction more rapidly than the mind can define it, yet the pleasure, the peculiar frisson of ambiguity

which attends the recognition of a trompe-l'oeil illusion, is primarily intellectual. The pleasure lies not in the moment of deception but in the discovery of the fraud; the momentary jolt to our perceptions of an accomplished visual trick is robbed of its threat as we smilingly acknowledge how cleverly we have been fooled.

There is a fifteenth-century painting titled *Portrait of the Artist and his Wife,* by the Master of Frankfurt, which amusingly clarifies the difference between realistic representation and trompe l'oeil. Husband and wife stand behind a table set with cherries on a plate, a jug of flowers, two bread rolls, and a knife. Though painted with technical assurance, and a fine double portrait, there is nothing at first glance about the picture to tease our preconceptions. Then one notices the fly, a blue-bottle poised on the wife's starched and snowy wimple. One's first reaction is that a real fly has settled on the picture, Denis' "plane surface." The trick and the joke lie in the juxtaposition of scale—a life-size fly on scaled-down portrait heads. But in the instant of pleasurably recognizing the deception, one becomes aware that the jeu d'esprit is more complex than that, the ambiguities in critical parlance, operating at many levels . . . because there is another, and larger, fly *in* the picture, painted in the act of sneaking up on the cherries by the rim of the plate. The second fly is almost twice the size of the first, trompe-l'oeil fly, and this disparity in scale reveals that the fly joke has a further purpose: to create depth within the picture so that the lady in the wimple becomes distanced by the simple device of showing

9

her insect (albeit outsize relative to her head) as much smaller than the brute crawling about in the foreground. What sharpens our enjoyment of these subtleties is the small sardonic glint in the steady gaze of the Master of Frankfurt observing us as we fall in and out of the visual traps he sprung so cleverly all those centuries ago.

If what art directors call "s,s," or same-scale representation, together with skillful perspective and a high degree of finish, are the sine qua non of successful painted illusionism, it is the wit and waggishness of the best examples which have made the genre so endearing and popular throughout its astonishingly long history. As Karen Chambers' devoted research amply confirms in this book, the art of trompe l'oeil has a lineage almost as long as the use of paint itself. It raised a smile under the Pharaohs, and issued a tongue-in-cheek warn-

ing to Roman litterbugs in the shape of a mosaic pavement known as *The Unswept Floor,* where scraps of debris from a Lucullan banquet—lobster claws, fruit kernels, and grapevine twigs—lie scattered, seemingly, about the floor.

Now that trompe l'oeil— usually abridged to "trompe" by the cognoscenti, who would *never* commit the common mistake of calling it trompe *d'oeil*—seems to have become annexed to the fine arts, a book like this is a timely reminder of just how distinguished earlier trompe l'oeil often was, judged simply as painting. The roll call is impressive—Veronese, Giotto, Borromini, Tiepolo, Andrea Pozzo, to name only a few of the masters who succumbed to the lure of pushing verisimilitude in paint to its limit—and then some. This was not the best of which they were capable, and yet the drollery of it all—posses of angels whooshing through an imag-

inary oculus or tiers of beldames peering over a painted balustrade—suggests that these virtuoso excursions must have been as enormously enjoyable to paint as they remain for us to contemplate.

Karen Chambers has chosen to adopt a pluralistic approach to the subject, so that "wood-grained" Formica and fun furs get a look along with the merry capriccios of the artistic greats. Her thesis is both plausible and entertainingly presented by means of a splendidly varied gallery of examples, ancient, modern, and postmodern. It makes for a stimulating visual journey all round. But what stays with me is a sense of release and delight in studying mischievous subversions of our conceptual baggage which are patently, and frankly, meant to be *enjoyed,* and by anyone and everyone.

Jocasta Innes
London, May 1991

A FEW WELL-CHOSEN OBJECTS, SET AGAINST
APPROPRIATELY ADORNED WALLS, CAN COM-
PLETELY TRANSFORM A ROOM. RALPH LAUREN
CAPTURES THE FEEL OF THE SOUTHWEST WITH
COLORFUL TEXTILES, DISPLAYED IN AN ADOBE
INTERIOR FILLED WITH ENGAGING ARTIFACTS.

INTRODUCTION:

MORE AND LESS THAN MEETS THE EYE

Illusionism as a concept can be relatively easy to define: Basically illusionism is an instance of what you see is not what you get. Yet what you get may be both more and/or less than what you bargained for, which is why it is so intriguing an element in home design. For example, at the estate Chatsworth in England a trompe-l'oeil painting of a violin hanging on a door is installed on a locked door to a music room. What we get is a perfect reproduction of the musical instrument, plausibly located, *and* the pleasure in realizing, after a moment, that it is all an illusion. What we do not get, of course, is a real violin on a real door. Certainly, the illusion is preferable.

There are innumerable tomes on the aesthetic questions raised by illusion versus reality, on the physics of perception, and the mechanics of

TROMPLOY, INC. HAS TURNED THIS HALLWAY INTO AN EXTRAVAGANZA OF COLOR AND ILLUSIONISTIC EFFECTS. THE RESULT IS BOTH GRAND AND AMUSING, AS A "SCRAP OF PAPER" PERMANENTLY LITTERS THE FLOOR.

optical deceptions. The techniques are known as trompe l'oeil (literally, fools the eyes) and faux (false). Regardless of the approach of the philosopher, scientist, or artist, the discussion always revolves around the discrepancy between what we see with our eyes and what we know with our minds.

Illusionism is about our perception of reality as communicated through our senses. While illusionism is most commonly thought of as visual in the realm of home design, it can also be tactile. For example, fake fur feels furry, whether in rug form or as a chair-covering material.

Adelbert Ames, Jr.'s experiments in perspective and perception illustrate how strongly we try to impose our will on visual phenomena. Ames made three peep shows of what seemed to be, from one angle, a tubular chair. When the "chairs" were seen from an-

14

THE WALL COVERINGS AND FABRICS MANUFACTURED BY ZUBER & CIE, ABOVE, REPRODUCE CLASSIC TROMPE-L'OEIL PATTERNS.

CERAMIC BUSHEL-BASKET CANISTERS BY FITZ & FLOYD, RIGHT, ARE FILLED TO THE TOP WITH A GREENGROCER'S BONANZA.

other angle, two of the three were revealed to be only *illusions* of chairs. The legs and back of one were skewed and distorted: The back extended and widened at the top and the legs converged in such a way that if they were to continue they would have ultimately met at one point. Even more amazing was the "chair" that consisted of a series of wires suspended in front of a painted backdrop that "became" a chair seat when viewed from the prescribed angle. In reality the wires were a jumble that never actually connected except illusionistically from that one vantage point.

The many modes of illusionism can be defined and explained, but its delight comes from our *misinterpretation* of reality. Illusionism is not merely realism although it encompasses realistic rendering. A prerequisite for illusionism is one-to-one scale or the willingness of viewers to adapt themselves to the scale of the object. A meticulously drawn and painted dollar bill is not, strictly speaking, illusionistic if it appears several feet long as in a painting by Tony King. However, if it is accurately scaled and colored and "appears" pasted on a canvas as some of William Harnett's did, then it may succeed in alarming the agents on the lookout for counterfeiters.

Illusionism also must exist in context. A realistic landscape painting is not necessarily illusionistic because the scale may be inaccurate and its frame announces that it is art. However, if that frame becomes an actual window frame, then the vista becomes illusionistic.

In the fine arts "truth to materials" has been touted in the twentieth century, much as realism (truth to appearances) had been until then. And yet illusionism has been pervasive throughout recorded history.

Illusionism in the dwelling

17

FOR CENTURIES THE OBJECT OF PAINTERS WAS TO CREATE AN IMPRESSION OF THREE-DIMENSIONAL SPACE. CURT ROYSTON SUBVERTS THIS NOTION WITH ARTISTIC INSTALLATIONS FEATURING OBJECTS PAINTED TO APPEAR FLAT, ABOVE. A LIVE MODEL MAKES US DO A DOUBLE-TAKE.

A DETAIL FROM A ROYSTON INSTALLATION, RIGHT, INCLUDES AN ACTUAL TELEPHONE AND CHAIR THAT ARE PAINTED. THE BRUSHSTROKES "FLATTEN" THE REAL OBJECTS.

place can be said to start with the prehistoric cave paintings where an image of the prey was painted on the cave wall as a charm to ensure a successful hunt. In the classic textbook on the history of art, *Gardner's Art Through the Ages*, the authors hypothesize that the prehistoric cave painter in France did not distinguish between "illusion and reality and that for him the bison recreated on the wall was different from the bison he hunted only in its state of being . . . hunters may have thrown spears at the images—as sharp gouges in the side of the bison at Niaux suggest. . . ."

The impulse to create decorative and architectural illusions within the home was felt by even the most ancient of cultures. The Egyptians painted ceilings like skies, the Greeks and Romans frescoed trompe-l'oeil vistas in their houses. Baroque artists perfected these illusionary games,

19

and contemporary artists have painted ersatz Baroque facades on blank walls.

It took until the twentieth century for artists to break away from realism. Picasso and Braque shattered our perception of what painting and sculpture were supposed to do by their fragmenting vision of reality. Yet, even as these Cubist masters were retreating from realism in their paintings, they were advancing toward a different type of realism. Their collages incorporated elements of the tangible world: cigarette packs, scraps cut from newspapers, and even a bit of oilcloth patterned after chair caning in Picasso's seminal work *Still Life with Chair Caning*, 1911–1912.

In the later twentieth century, in a new twist on the art-for-art's-sake tradition, artists have begun to appropriate other artists' images for their own original artwork. This move plays havoc with the con-

cept of plagiarism. When Mike Bidlo paints a copy of one of Picasso's well-known paintings, how do we evaluate his contribution to aesthetic history? Is what he is doing any different from what the Chinese artist Song Bin does in a cramped Hong Kong studio when he reproduces, by the hundreds, Leonardo's *Mona Lisa* for a mail order catalog?

Illusionism extends beyond the fine arts. In the home, it can act as a decorative device, whether it's a faux granite finish on a bathroom tub, a painted but realistic-looking archway, or plastic tumblers that appear to be sculpted from stone.

Roughly speaking illusionism has been the means to three ends throughout history: economy, practicality, and entertainment. The latter encompasses a desire to amuse oneself and others, an ambition to emulate fashion, and a nostalgic yearning to re-create

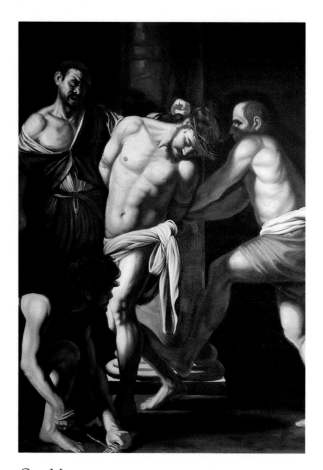

OLD MASTER PAINTINGS ARE OUT OF THE BUDGET RANGE OF ALL BUT MILLIONAIRES TODAY. THOSE WITH MORE MODEST BANK ACCOUNTS ACQUIRE IMAGINATIVE REPRODUCTIONS LIKE THIS ONE INSPIRED BY CARAVAGGIO, ABOVE. PAINTED BY ALBERT POPA, IT IS AVAILABLE THROUGH PAXWELL PAINTING STUDIOS, INC.

EVERYTHING ABOUT KEUNG SZETO'S <u>LITTLE</u> <u>BUTTERFLY</u>, ABOVE, SEEMS REAL; THE INSECT ITSELF APPEARS TO HAVE JUST ALIGHTED ON THE SURFACE. IN REALITY, THE SCENE IS ONLY ACRYLIC PAINT ON LINEN.

another time or place. Since nothing about illusionism is straightforward, these reasons naturally overlap.

Without going into a technical explanation of how illusionism succeeds in fooling our eyes and minds, I can state that it relies on three basic strategies: imitation, reproduction, and re-creation. These may be considered artificial categories and, like the reasons for illusionism, are not mutually exclusive. For our purposes, imitation refers to the raw materials of illusionism: leopard-printed velvet, aluminum siding, vinyl floor covering imprinted with a stone pattern, wood-grained Formica, and the like. Reproduction describes objects such as Louis XIV armchairs made in the twentieth century, wax fruit, and copies of Chanel suits. Both imitation and reproduction can contribute to a re-creation, illusion on the large scale and, when not histori-

21

cally correct, more properly *al-lusionism*. The endless exciting and witty ways that illusionism enlivens the home fill the chapters of this book. The variety of images presented are meant to inspire the home designer to create personalized settings that venture beyond ordinary room design.

22

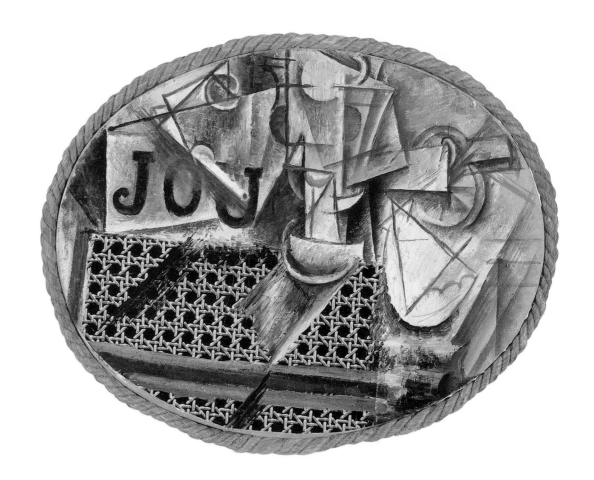

FATHER OF THE COLLAGE TECHNIQUE, PICASSO INCORPORATED A BIT OF OILCLOTH PATTERNED AS CHAIR CANING IN STILL LIFE WITH CHAIR CANING, 1911–1912, ABOVE. THE FRAME IS A PIECE OF REAL ROPE.

Tony King's paintings of currency could not possibly be mistaken for the real thing because of their larger-than-life size and imaginative colors. Black Washington, above, measures more than three by eight feet and is sparked by bright colors against a dramatic black background.

I

I

26

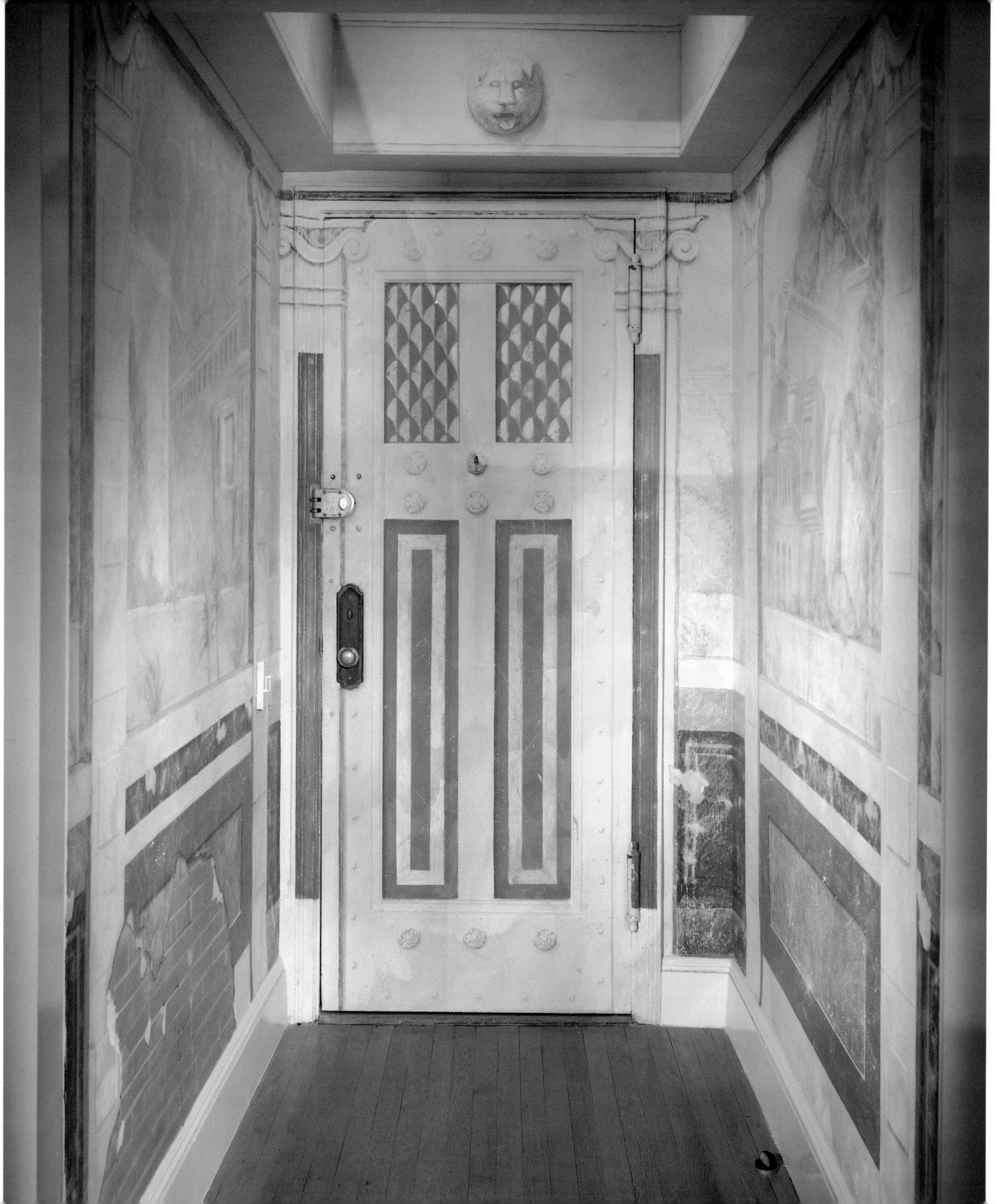

DELIGHTFUL DECEPTIONS

In spite of the word and the vision it conjures up, illusionism is not all done with mirrors. It is achieved in three very concrete ways: imitation, reproduction, and re-creation.

Usually imitation is the use of one material to simulate the effect of another. Faux finishes, synthetic materials, and even trompe-l'oeil techniques all *imitate* reality. Imitative as well as authentic materials can then be used to make objects that *reproduce* other objects. When they utilize "false" materials, they become doubly illusionistic. A reproduction replicates an original artifact whether it is a perfectly ripe apple made in wax, a mallard duck carved in wood, or an Empire console made a century and a half after the fact. A re-creation may involve both of these techniques in its creation, but it operates on a large scale—environmentally. Imitations and reproduc-

ARTIST DAVID FISCH ILLUMINATED AN ENTRY HALL WITH A PAINTED SKYLIGHT CONSTANTLY STREAMING WITH SUNLIGHT. THE HALLWAY'S FAUX MARBRE PATTERN IS REMINISCENT OF THE MOTIFS OF POMPEII.

tions may be part of a re-creation although the original materials and objects can be utilized. For example, wood-grained Formica is an *imitation* of wood. When it is used to surface your kitchen cabinets, the *cabinets* become *reproductions* of actual wooden cabinets. If you use "wood" fiberboard paneling, essentially a photographic imitation of wood, to reproduce François I's own illusionistically grain-painted "cypress"-panelled room at Fontainebleau, you are *re-creating* the grandeur of another time.

The extent to which such design approaches succeed depends upon the willingness of the knowing viewer (or the gullibility of the uninformed one) to believe in the effect. Who would not be seduced by the idea of relaxing in a room graced with marble floors and columns? Upon closer inspection, we learn that these grand materials are merely painted

surfaces, but their effect is hardly diminished by this discovery.

Throughout the centuries nearly every material has been imitated. Stone was carved to resemble reed matting and palm logs in ancient Egyptian temples, but more often other materials have been used to imitate stone. Stucco and concrete have been fashioned into three-dimensional imitations

THE SON OF AN EASTERN EUROPEAN MASTER CRAFTSMAN, THOMAS MASARYK CARRIES ON A TRADITION OF DESIGN INTEGRITY. HE PAINTED THE WALLS OF THIS BATHROOM IN A FAUX MARBRE PATTERN AND EVEN MIMICKED MOSAICS TO ESTABLISH A SENSE OF THE PAST, ABOVE.

MASARYK'S ARTISTRY EXTENDS TO EVERY CORNER OF THE BATH, RIGHT, TRANSFORMING IT INTO THE KIND OF SYBARITIC RETREATS ENJOYED BY ROMAN STATESMEN, BUT ENHANCED BY MODERN PLUMBING.

of stone since Roman times. Before 3000 B.C. the Egyptians imitated speckled red granite in paint, probably beginning the venerable history of faux finishes. Between 2300 and 2000 B.C., the Minoan ancestors of the Greeks "marbleized" pottery. Like the Greek and Roman wall paintings of faux marbre, the dadoes of Roman basilicas and later of Early Christian and Romanesque churches were painted as the luxury stone. Fifteenth-century Renaissance Florentine painters renovated the gray stone interiors of Gothic structures by inserting inner shells of plaster painted as inlaid "marble." Today we find advertisements in magazines filled with notices of contemporary artisans eager to transform our baths into extravagant marble-lined rooms for the cost of the paint and their labor.

Not in all cases is the goal to faithfully reproduce the look of marble economically. When

CONGOLEUM'S STONEGATE VINYL PATTERN RE-
PRODUCES THE EFFECT OF STONE PAVING, YET IS
SOFTER UNDERFOOT AND EASIER TO MAINTAIN
THAN THE REAL THING.

we strive to create such effects in the home, we follow in a grand historic tradition. Luigi Barzini in *The Italians* says that "half the marble one sees in churches or patrician palazzi is, in fact, but smooth plaster deceptively painted . . . Inevitably, the Italians are tempted to applaud more those performances, which stray dangerously farthest from reality, those which make do with the scantiest materials, those which do not even pretend to imitate existing models and still manage to be effective, convincing, stirring, or entertaining." At the late medieval Palazzo Vecchio and Santa Croce in Florence, the wainscotting was painted to resemble pastel marble, but in a highly stylized and expressionistic manner, confirming Barzini's observation. In the provinces this more abstract "marbling" also delighted viewers. An American example of such techniques applied to

the home is the 1725 "William and Mary parlour" from a Massachusetts house and now in the Winterthur Museum, Delaware. The woodwork is painted in hyperkinetic swirls of faux pink marble and wood that are exuberantly false.

To effect grandeur is always one of the main reasons for faux marbre finishes. When it is patently false, the viewer's reaction is also tinged with amusement. Many contemporary products rely on that response. Every picnicker knows the value of paper plates. For those who don't wish to forego elegance for practicality, there are faux granite or marble plates and paper napkins.

Iron has been cast to imitate classical stone columns and aluminum extruded to imitate wood siding for houses. Fluid "draperies" have been painted on flat and solid stone walls as the Pompeiians did or carved in unyielding plaster as Sir John Soane did for his early

THESE BLOWN-GLASS FRUITS ARE GLORIOUS
STAND-INS FOR THE EDIBLE ORIGINALS. SEAT-
TLE-BASED ARTISTS FLORA C. MACE AND JOEY
KIRKPATRICK CREATED THEM TO "HELP US TO
RECOGNIZE THE CELEBRATORY ASPECTS OF EV-
ERYDAY LIFE."

nineteenth-century London town house. Leather has been imitated by embossed wallpapers in the eighteenth century and a fake leather was the original aim of the inventor of linoleum in the nineteenth century. It has been successfully simulated by plastics in the twentieth. Real furs and skins now compete with synthetic "fun furs"—whether used as throw rugs or chair coverings—and animals lend their patterns in trompe-l'oeil silk screen or weaving techniques to a variety of nonfurry surfaces.

Reproductions of objects abound, whether they are made of porcelain (such as the fruits and vegetables made in Strasbourg to grace eighteenth-century dining tables) or of glass (such as the glass fruits blown by contemporary glass artists Flora Mace and Joey Kirkpatrick). Fragile flowers have been immortalized in a variety of materials, from costly jade in Asia to elegant silk designs found in oversize arrangements in the home; battered leather bags, paper sacks, and craggy rocks have all been convincingly fashioned in clay. In the hands of a skillful carver, wood has been whittled into bicycles, delicate flowers, and even a leather jacket hanging on a hall tree. Also illusionistic are reproductions of period furniture pieces. Authentic Louis XIV pieces may not be affordable for the general public, but cut-rate furniture showrooms offer royal splendor for workman's wages.

Stylistic revivals offer us the chance to re-create another era and are a regular component of the history of the fine and applied arts.

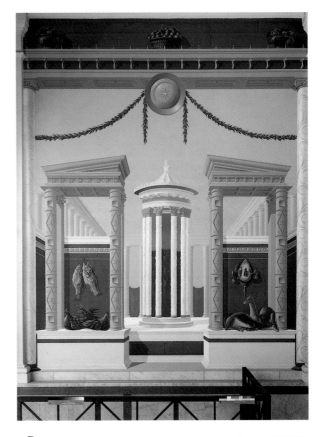

ROMAN MURAL PAINTING IS RE-CREATED WITH REMARKABLE AUTHENTICITY AT THE J. PAUL GETTY MUSEUM IN MALIBU, CALIFORNIA. LIKE THEIR ANCIENT COUNTERPARTS, THE CONTEMPORARY MURALISTS USED ELEMENTS OF CLASSICAL ARCHITECTURE IN THE DESIGNS. ON A LESS AMBITIOUS LEVEL, SUCH MOTIFS CAN EMBELLISH THE ORDINARY HOME.

IMITATION: THE GREAT IMPOSTERS

THE NINETEENTH-CENTURY AMERICAN TROMPE-L'OEIL ARTIST WILLIAM HARNETT WAS A VIRTUOSO WITH PAINT, ABLE TO CREATE CONVINCINGLY A VARIETY OF EFFECTS CALCULATED TO AMAZE HIS VIEWERS. EVERY OBJECT IN THIS PAINTING HAS A PALPABLE PRESENCE.

Imitation may be the sincerest form of flattery but its intentions are usually somewhat different. For our purposes, it is often the means to an end and will refer to illusionistic effects that are generally components of something larger.

One of the most effective illusionistic techniques is described by the French term "trompe l'oeil"—literally translated as "fool the eye." Trompe-l'oeil artists intend to puzzle, mystify, and entertain. We are surprised and deceived at the sight of a trompe-l'oeil painting or object. What we see appears to be a part of our familiar world and often we may even reach out to test its reality.

Trompe-l'oeil techniques have been employed to imitate practically everything to be found in the natural world. Infinite varieties of marble and other stones, wood, cloth, leather, fur, flowers, leaves, even living creatures, if their stillness can be plausibly explained, have been faithfully reproduced in paint.

Trompe l'oeil can extend to three dimensions, but when it does it becomes, by our definitions, reproduction. For the moment, let us confine ourselves to two dimensions.

While the fluidity of fabric does not seem to make a likely candidate for simulation by trompe-l'oeil techniques, it nevertheless has been ingeniously imitated. In the fourth century B.C., the Greek painter Parrhasius is said to have painted a curtain so realistically that his rival, Apelles, was fooled. At the Palazzo Davanzati in Florence in 1395, the "tapestries" lining the wedding chamber of Francesco di Tommaso Davizzi and Catelana degli Alberti were part of an elaborate trompe l'oeil that included a loggia opening on to a garden above the drapery.

THE LOOK OF MARBLE AND GRANITE, ABOVE, IS PRODUCED WITH EASE BY ATLANTA DECORATIVE PAINTER SCOTT WATERMAN.

NEW YORK ARTIST TOM ISBELL IS ABLE TO CREATE A LUXURIOUS GOLD-VEINED MARBLE THAT ADDS A CLASSICAL NOTE TO ANY SETTING, RIGHT. IN DOING SO, HE CONTINUES A TRADITION DATING FROM EGYPTIAN TIMES.

The drapery, elaborately patterned with heraldic devices, hangs from rings fastened to the parapet of the loggia and covers the walls. It is pulled back at the corners of the room to reveal a rich lining.

While most theater curtains are real drapery, the Paris Opera's curtain designed by Jean Louis Charles Garnier in 1874 was not. The two-dimensional surface of the flat curtain was painted to resemble an elaborately draped and tasseled curtain in an ironic trompe-l'oeil rendition.

Author and trompe-l'oeil artist Martin Battersby points out the entertainment quality of this deception, which prefigures the fantasies that would be revealed when the "seemingly cumbrous weight of fabric was effortlessly lifted."

Printed wallpapers have imitated textiles. In fact, the first wallpapers manufactured in England in the sixteenth century were intended to simulate the brocades and velvets popular as wall coverings. Soon after wallpaper makers took embroidery, leather, and even gathered drapery as their models. In the nineteenth century trompe-l'oeil wallpapers were praised and promoted by Charles Blanc, director of the Beaux-Arts in 1848 and 1870 and author of the influential text, *Grammaire des Arts Décoratifs*. He claimed the nation's newest manufacturing techniques lent a "simple sheet of paper not only the brilliance of silk and satin, the stiffness of moiré, the still colors of cloth and felt, the polish of ceramic glazes, but the grain of a material, the very stitch of old tapestries, the thickness of crocheted embroideries, the deep embossing of Spanish leather, the punctuated swelling of brocatelle, and even the bulge of the padded stuff."

The same strategies are in use today; flocked wallpapers are still available and popular.

THIS NEOCLASSICAL DRAPE, ABOVE AND RIGHT, WAS INSPIRED BY A NINETEENTH-CENTURY FRENCH WALLPAPER. IT HANGS IN FRONT OF A LUXURIOUS "MALACHITE" DOOR. EVERYTHING IS REALISTICALLY RENDERED IN PAINT BY THE CONTEMPORARY TROMPE-L'OEILIST SCOTT WATERMAN.

Other textile sources are also used. Brunschwig & Fils produces a *Hare and Hound Border* based on a set of eighteenth-century crewel-embroidered bedhangings in the collection of the Winterthur Museum.

Contemporary trompe-l'oeil painters still create extravagant and rich effects of drapery. In a New York apartment house, James Alan Smith has evoked a sense of luxury by lining three sides of a mundane metal elevator cab with a "swagged linen" above a "wooden dado." David Cohn has created a windblown pavilion with a rippling canvas roof for a seaside house designed by decorator David Barrett. Scott Waterman has painted a single panel of white drapery over a dressing room door that is itself painted in a faux malachite. The architect Michael Graves has decorated buildings with gigantic swags of "sculpted" drapery.

Wood is another familiar

PASSENGERS IN THIS ELEVATOR CAB BECOME TIME TRAVELLERS AS THEY EXPERIENCE JAMES ALLEN SMITH'S EFFECT OF NEOCLASSICAL DRAPERY AND TRADITIONAL WOODEN WAINSCOTTING.

material that has a long history of being imitated. Sometimes it has merely been enhanced through a technique known as wood graining (painting wood to imitate the grain and coloration of other more exotic and expensive woods). There are two schools of thought on realism in wood graining. One advocates a highly naturalistic rendering, and it is usually the attitude of the artisan using the technique to enhance a cheaper wood, for example, transforming pine into rosewood. The other school prefers a more fantastic approach, one that is more entertaining. An early nineteenth-century English wood grainer compared graining to portraiture: "The humble art of imitating woods and marbles is in some measure allied to the high art of portrait-painting." The grainer must depend upon his "natural genius" to avoid the common fault of "producing a caricature of the object of which he attempts to produce a correct resemblance."

At the same time household expert J. C. Loudon in 1833 argued for an artful abstraction in wood graining. Imitative woodwork, he asserted, should be painted not to have "the imitation mistaken for the original, but rather to create an allusion to it."

Wood graining has been done since the First Dynasty of Egypt. Because of that country's dry climate, wood was a rare commodity and had to be imported from Syria, making it a precious material. It was common to enhance its surface with false graining. Throughout the seventeenth and eighteenth centuries "cedar" and "mahogany" were grained on fir, which was easily disguised, as a fashionable and cost-conscious replacement for oak paneling in England. In the eighteenth century, rather than go to the expense of importing bamboo from the Far East, where it was plentiful and therefore cheap, Europeans imitated it for the fashionable Chinoiserie furniture. Craftsmen imitated the scarce material with turned and painted wood and plaster of paris joint.

Nineteenth-century Neoclassical architects had rosewood and mahogany grained over pine in Europe, while in the provinces of the New World, furniture makers also imitated rosewood on pine in an economical move. Even the Shakers, not known for embellishment, occasionally enhanced their cherry pieces with more elaborate cherry wood graining.

Invented by the Formica Insulation Company in the 1920s, plastic laminates have become today's ubiquitous substitute for wood. They are both economical and practical, but consumers have also been assured that Formica is also suitable for use in elegant surroundings. A 1948 advertise-

THIS COLONIAL AMERICAN WOODEN CHEST IS DECORATED IN AN IMPRESSIONISTIC FAUX MARBRE PATTERN. THE NAIVE, UNFINISHED QUALITY ONLY ADDS TO ITS CHARM, AS IT DOES NOT ATTEMPT TO REPRODUCE MARBLE FAITHFULLY BUT RENDER IT MORE FANCIFULLY.

ment promised consumers that "Beauty Bonded Formica Real-wood" was always at home, whether in "the Luxury Liner's 'showplace' or the clean, colorful charm of Mrs. America's own kitchen and dinette," emphasizing both the prestige and the practicality of the adaptable imposter.

Formica—the grandfather of all plastic laminates—has become so much a part of our environment that we almost accept it as real. It represents itself almost as much as it does the materials it imitates. It is essentially a sandwich of resin-soaked paper sheets topped with a lithographed picture of wood or whatever pattern it is intended to imitate. The layers are fused together into a single sheet by baking it under 1,400 pounds of pressure per square inch. Formica and its offspring appear everywhere, prepared to imitate any surface pattern practically and economically.

The skills of the trompe-

FORMICA CAN REPRODUCE EXACTLY ANY PATTERN FOUND IN NATURE, BUT OFTEN WITH BETTER PERFORMANCE FEATURES. THESE CABINETS ARE MORE ECONOMICAL AND PRACTICAL THAN THEIR WOOD COUNTERPARTS.

l'oeil painter, so crucial for creating effective faux surfaces such as marbleizing and wood graining, have also been used to create extravagant architectural settings or even to enhance nature. The eruption of Mount Vesuvius in A.D. 79 preserved for eternity the towns of Pompeii and Herculaneum, giving us an accurate view of Roman daily life at the beginning of the Christian era. The fashion at the time was to face walls with thin slabs of marble, creating the appearance of solid marble. For those unable to afford this, there was paint on plaster, which effectively simulated real stone, popular from 200 to 60 B.C. Later (60–20 B.C.) painted features, such as columns, pilasters, and window frames, elaborated on these deceptions to create a false architecture. Through the "windows" one could see distant views of landscapes and cities. These were painted with a flickering play of light and dark so that viewers believed they were looking at an *actual* landscape through a *real* window. While Roman execution of this was a little awkward because of their ignorance of perspective and the optics of color, the results were nevertheless charming and effective. This illusionistic strategy was refined in the Renaissance, exploited by the Mannerists, and reached perfection during the Baroque period.

In the fifteenth century at the Castle of Issogne, Aosta, Italy, in the Hall of the Barons, Corinthian-type columns of rock crystal and porphyry alternate with panels of fine brocades to "frame" a view of Jerusalem and Golgotha. Painted by unknown artists, the architecture of the Holy City is outlined and the drawings of the exotic animals and haloed figures are stilted, like cardboard cutouts placed in slits in the background. However, the overall effect is that of looking

TROMPLOY, INC. HAS TRANSFORMED THIS DINING ROOM INTO A ROMANESQUE FANTASY WITH HEAVY MASONRY WALLS AND ROUNDED ARCHES. A VIEW OF AN ITALIAN-INSPIRED LANDSCAPE OPENS UP THE ROOM ILLUSIONISTICALLY. NEOCLASSICAL URNS SIT ON THE FAUX MARBRE LEDGE.

through a "real" colonnade to a "real" landscape.

About a century later the work of Renaissance artist Baldassare Peruzzi (1481–1536) in the Hall of Perspectives in the Villa Farnesina in Rome (1512) was more convincing: A viewer was apt to truly believe that the scene of Rome glimpsed through a double row of "marble" pillars was "real." The secrets of perspective had been discovered and were at the service of the trompe-l'oeil artist. The painting expands the room as the marble flooring is extended illusionistically by a part of the wall painting.

The Mannerist period is thought by some to be a continuation of the Renaissance. It takes the artistic developments of the Renaissance to the point of exaggeration, even caricature. They become "mannered." It was a period that valued the bizarre, always a congenial atmosphere for

ZULEYKA BENITEZ'S FAUX MARBRE EFFECTS ARE EXUBERANT. IN PLAYFUL FASHION, SHE PLACES A GREEN MARBLE GLOBE ON A BALUSTRADE, CHALLENGING THE REALITY OF THE FLATNESS OF THE WALL, ABOVE.

ROOMS NEVER NEED TO BE CONFINING, AS DECORATIVE PAINTER TOM ISBELL PROVES WITH THIS CLOUD-FILLED SKY, LEFT. A MIRRORED TABLE CONTRIBUTES TO THE EXPANSIVENESS OF THE SETTING BY REFLECTING LIGHT.

trompe l'oeil. A striking example of Mannerist illusionism is the Palazzo del Tè, which was designed and decorated for the duke of Mantua as an extravagant pleasure palace by the architect and painter Giulio Romano. His *Fall of the Giants* is described by the trompe-l'oeil scholar M. L. d'Otrange Mastai "as a sixteenth-century equivalent of a Cecil B. De Mille set." Enormous and ferocious figures pull down massive columns leaving the viewer convinced the roof will cave in momentarily. The illusion is aided by the beehive construction of the room, which eliminates all awkward corners that would disrupt the perspective.

Perhaps the grandest example of architectural illusionism is the ceiling of the Church of Saint Ignatius in Rome. Following in the tradition begun in ancient Egypt of dematerializing ceilings by painting the sky on them, the Jesuit priest and painter Andrea Pozzo (1642–

THIS WOOD MARQUETRY LI-
QUOR CABINET, RIGHT, WAS DE-
SIGNED BY PETER FORBES AND
PATRICK HICKOX AND BUILT BY
JAMIE ROBERTSON. IT COM-
BINES CARVED MOLDING WITH
AN ILLUSIONISTIC COFFERED
CEILING, CREATED WITH DIF-
FERENT COLORED BLOCKS OF
WOOD INLAID TO CREATE A
CONVINCING PERSPECTIVE.

PART OF AN UNDERGROUND PARKING GARAGE
HAS BEEN TURNED INTO AN "OPEN-AIR" WINE
CELLAR, ABOVE. SCOTT WATERMAN TRANS-
FORMED THE CEILING OF THE GARAGE, WHICH
SUPPORTS THIRTY STORIES OF CONDOMINIUMS,
INTO A PERMANENT BLUE SKY WITH WISPY
CLOUDS. A HIDDEN TAPE DECK PLAYS GRE-
GORIAN CHANTS, ADDING AN AUDITORY ELE-
MENT TO THE ILLUSION.

1709) "opened" the ceiling to the heavens so that Christ bearing the Cross becomes the source of all light. The 1685 work, which also features Saint Ignatius, his followers, and angels all levitating, is a tour de force, even if it requires the viewer to stand at one particular spot to get the full effect.

Other materials can also be used to achieve trompe-l'oeil effects. Around the 1460s a wood marquetry technique was developed by the Landinara brothers. They inlaid delicately shaded pieces of wood to create amazingly realistic renditions of still-life subjects. During the Middle Ages and Renaissance the private studies of the aristocracy were often set apart from the rest of the house and decorated especially to create an atmosphere conducive to contemplation, and wood intarsia was often used to panel them during the Renaissance. In the Renaissance *studiolo* of Federigo da

Montefeltro, duke of Urbino, created by Francesco di Giorgio Martini (1439–1502) and Baccio Pontelli (1450–1495), half-opened cupboards reveal books, papers, musical and scientific instruments, all of the accoutrements of the scholarly life. The tonality of the wood, from ivory to deep brown, bathes the room in an amber glow that moves the eye over the details quickly, easily, and uncritically. This technique, intarsia, is still being used in Paris by the Jansen workshop. Although less elaborate, a contemporary example of the tradition is a liquor cabinet, designed by Peter Forbes and Patrick Hickox and crafted by Jamie Robertson. A coffered hallway surrounds the central cabinet flanked with pilasters and a broken pediment—the depth all an illusion.

The pelts of endangered species show up as "fun-fur coats" at discount chains like K mart and Marks and Spencer

FORMICA CABINETS, ABOVE, RE-PRODUCE WOOD GRAIN WHILE THE COUNTERTOPS ARE A PURE PRIMARY COLOR.

ARTIST THOMAS MASARYK USES A FAUX FINISH ON AN OTHER-WISE ORDINARY WALL, RIGHT.

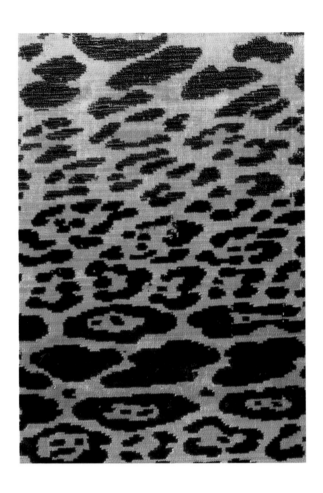

THE 1920S SPAWNED A RAGE FOR EXOTIC ANIMAL SKINS. THIS CONTEMPORARY VELVET BY BRUNSCHWIG & FILS, NEAR LEFT, CONTINUES THE TRADITION WITHOUT HARMING ENDANGERED SPECIES AND AT A REDUCED COST.

THE POOLSIDE ROOM OF THIS FLORIDA HOUSE IS GLAMOURIZED BY FAKE FUR THROWS AND PILLOWS, LEFT. THE COMBINED EFFECT OF THE FABRIC, WICKER FURNITURE, AND LUSH PLANTINGS CREATES A FEEL OF TROPICAL SPLENDOR.

as well as more expensive department stores like Harrod's and Bloomingdale's, on dancers' leotards and tights, as blouses and skirts worn by suburban matrons as well as punk rockers from London and New York's East Village. At home you can have leopard-spotted sheets and comforter or cover your floor with an "ocelot" carpet. Terry cloth bath towels mimic the rugs made from trophies of big-game safaris: tigers, leopards, and zebras. All these imitations neatly sidestep the volatile issues of endangered species and animal rights.

Imitation is but one of the tricks in the illusionist's repertoire. It is used to package reality more attractively, exotically, or luxuriously. It is a strategy of what you see is what you get but what you actually get may not be what you thought you got. Get it?

REPRODUCTION: A NATURAL ACT

Sometimes what you get is pretty tangible. When that is the case, what you probably got from the illusionist is a reproduction. When made to the same scale as the original, it is a counterfeit.

Copies are always manufactured in response to market demand. One licensee of Batman memorabilia, a hot item in 1989 with the release of the blockbuster film, explains that "bootlegging spreads when there's a shortage of goods."

Such fakery raises the question of counterfeit money; throughout the centuries, fine artists and designers have always naturally gravitated toward representing currency in their work. Paintings that illusionistically represent paper money go back as far as the eighteenth century in Europe. Many stories are told of nineteenth-century American trompe-l'oeil painters running

THE APPLE SHAPE MAKES A PERFECT FORM FOR THESE FITZ & FLOYD JARS. EVEN WHEN NOT STORING TREATS, THEY ARE CHARMING OBJECTS FOR ADORNING SHELVES AND TABLES.

afoul of the United States Treasury Department for their depictions of bank notes. The appearance of counterfeit bills in circulation that were meticulously hand-painted, by a counterfeiter known as Jim the Penman, caused U.S. Treasury agents to make calls on William Harnett, J. D. Chalfant, John Haberle, and others whenever their paintings of money were displayed. Chalfant's Philadelphia dealer James Earle wrote in September 1888 to say that he had a buyer for Chalfant's *Perfect Counterfeit*, but wanted to be assured that "we will be quite free from investigation or injunction by the United States Government."

More recently in England a young American artist, J.S.G. Boggs, was tried for "reproducing" British currency. Like his American antecedents, he had no intention of circulating his drawings as real money. Rather, he used them for an

WHAT WAS ONCE AN ORDINARY BATHROOM BECAME A MEDIEVAL FANTASY SETTING THROUGH SKILLFUL APPLICATION OF PAINT. TROMPLOY, INC. CREATED THE EFFECT OF THICK STONE WALLS, MADE WHIMSICAL BY A VIEW INTO A RUSTIC COTTAGE GARDEN.

INSPIRED BY A CHINESE RED LACQUER CABINET, THIS MEDIA STORAGE UNIT BY HENREDON CONCEALS TWENTIETH-CENTURY ENTERTAINMENT PARAPHERNALIA, WHICH LOOKS SO OUT OF PLACE IN A CONTEMPORARY ROOM.

unusual form of barter: He drew bank notes and exchanged them at face value for goods and services. He estimated that he had "spent" thirty-five thousand dollars before his arrest in 1986. The jury eventually acquitted Boggs despite what seemed to be an overwhelming case against him. The foreman of the jury confessed that they had "loved his work."

Reproductions fuel the furniture industry. A walk through any furniture showroom from the most expensive to the most cut-rate will reveal that there is a market for reproduction furniture. We can identify with the patriots of the American Revolution and sit in Windsor chairs or replicate the splendor of Versailles with a Louis XIV bedroom suite. Chippendale, Hepplewhite, and Sheraton can furnish modest homes. Or if we are handy, we can put together a Shaker chair or a Queen Anne dining room from kits that are available. It seems as though any style popular enough to be remembered can be acquired in reproduction.

New York Times interior design writer Carol Vogel characterized the predominant theme at a recent International Home Furnishings Market in High Point, North Carolina, as nostalgia. The showrooms featured Victorian, Biedermeier, and century-old Russian styles. Also, the Baker Furniture Company introduced a small line based on furniture from the Royal Pavilion at Brighton, a delightful, highly romanticized *re-creation* of the Orient, designed by John Nash for the prince regent, later George IV. Completed in 1821, Brighton was an exotic seaside folly, Hindu on the outside and Chinese on the inside, and a good example of how nineteenth-century consumers played out their fantasies on a large scale. The oriental flavor of Brighton was far from au-

thentic; it was, in fact, illusionistic according to our definition. The Baker line then becomes doubly so as it reproduces what was already an illusionistic re-creation.

Designer Ralph Lauren has created an empire based on illusionism. Throughout the 1980s, his clothing designs offered us a chance to project the look of "old money classicism" or the ruggedness of the American West. With Lauren's entry into the home furnishings market, he became a set de-

USING A TECHNIQUE CALLED PÂTE-DE-VERRE (WHICH TRANSLATES LITERALLY FROM THE FRENCH AS "PASTE OF GLASS"), THE AMERICAN ARTIST DOUG ANDERSON FILLS MOLDS MADE FROM ACTUAL OBJECTS WITH POWDERED GLASS TO CAST HIS AMAZINGLY LIFELIKE SCULPTURES—CASUAL ENOUGH TO LOOK AT HOME IN THE MOST HUMBLE SETTINGS. THEIR WAXY TEXTURE AND PASTEL SHADES REVEAL THE ARTIST'S DECEPTION, ABOVE.

WENDELL CASTLE NOT ONLY CARVED THIS COATRACK FROM MAHOGANY BUT ALSO THE "SOFT" FELT HAT AND SCARF THAT HANG FROM IT. TO FURTHER THE ILLUSION, ACTUAL HATS, SCARVES, AND A JACKET OR TWO COULD BE HUNG ALONGSIDE, RIGHT.

signer as well, introducing Navaho-inspired and other tartan blankets, Santa Fe-style accessories, and other objects that re-create another time or place in the home.

Absolute verisimilitude is not always the goal of artists and designers who reproduce objects. Often a model is replicated in material that may be quite foreign to the original. The form may be faithfully reproduced but the material is allowed to assert itself. The kick for the viewers comes when they realize that something is not quite right. The object may be rigid where the original is yielding, or it may not be the right texture or the expected color. Paper bags have been realistically rendered in clay by Michel Harvey as well as the Rosenthal Studio-Line. The sacks by both makers stand rigidly with every wrinkle and crinkle accurately rendered. M&Co. has produced a delightful paper-

weight made to look like a crumpled sheet torn from a yellow legal pad. If it were really paper, it could never perform its task. The object's irony makes us smile. Another ceramic artist, Richard Shaw, has created astonishingly realistic still lifes of books, crockery, and other common home objects. All are slip-cast in porcelain and either decaled or china-painted to meticulously imitate their models. A house of clay cards stands ready to collapse at any moment. The danger, known to the sophisticated viewer, is that these cards will shatter, not merely tumble should they fall. Of course, that danger is also an illusion since the cards are securely attached one to another.

The sculptor and furniture maker Wendell Castle produced a series of sculptures in the mid-1970s using furniture forms combined with trompe-l'oeil renderings in wood of objects you would expect to

see with them: a leather jacket on a hall tree, keys and gloves on a table, a hat on a chair. The wood is never disguised but nonetheless there is a moment when we nearly mistake the wooden umbrella or fedora or loaf of French bread for reality, not a representation.

A precursor of Wendell Castle, Rupert Carabin, carved a series of rather bizarre pieces of furniture that incorporated full-scale female nudes in the 1890s in Paris. One chair from 1896 features a woman attached to the back of the chair and two cats which serve as armrests.

Coming back to the present, Fumio Yoshimura's carved wood replicas never deny their material but the handling is so precise and correct that the viewer is amazed by the deception. His *Three Bicycles*, carved in linden, are completely realistic in detailing from the slender spokes to the chains to the brake cables curving over the handlebars. Even a cloth pennant seems capable of fluttering in the breeze.

Thomas Buechner, former president of Steuben Glass as well as founding director of the Corning Museum of Glass, has called glass the great pretender. The malleability of the medium makes it a perfect candidate to be molded into exquisitely realistic renditions of the natural world and can impart many moods to a room. Glass artist Doug Anderson uses molds made from the actual objects and then casts them using the pâte-de-verre, or paste of glass, technique. His subjects often come from nature: fish, delicate leaves, acorns, anything he finds in the woods. The powdered glasses fuse together to produce delicately colored sculptures that appear to be absolutely real except for the hue and texture, a waxy consistency. Anderson favors softened pastels fading from

DANIEL DOUKE'S <u>McMANUS, McMANUS, McMANUS</u> LOOKS LIKE A PACKAGE READY TO BE OPENED, BUT IT IS ALL AN ILLUSION OF PAINT ON CANVAS, ABOVE.

RICHARD LOWELL NEAS RECALLS THE CHINOISERIE FAD OF THE LAST CENTURY WITH TROMPE-L'OEIL BAMBOO WALLPAPER. THE DOOR IS PAINTED AND "COMBED" TO APPEAR TO BE PART WOVEN REED AND PART WOOD IN KEEPING WITH THE ORIENTAL MOTIF, RIGHT.

mauves to chartreuses or other equally lovely but unnatural combinations.

Glass's sister medium, clay, is also well suited to assuming organic forms and bringing a dynamic quality to interiors. Since the sixteenth century a genre of ceramic work has existed that reproduces fruits and vegetables. It was considered highly amusing in the seventeenth and eighteenth centuries to place dishes of fake food alongside the edible or to use food forms for functional serving dishes. Dining tables were set with soup tureens in the form of uncooked cabbage or bundles of asparagus; tea was poured from cabbage pots. Jacob Petit's vegetable dish and cover, circa 1850, are a "woven basket" topped by a still life of abundance: asparagus, scallions, carrots, gourds, and more. Adrien Dalpayrat (1844–1910) made a pitcher in the form of a gourd in 1892–1895 and Taxile Doat

(1851–1938) used the same inspiration for his bottle in 1903. Both were made in stoneware. Larger companies also used natural forms such as the fennel coffee service produced by Sevres at the beginning of the twentieth century.

In nineteenth-century France, this joke extended to the reproduction of the plausible in clearly nonrealistic materials including metal. Christofle et Cie. made a chestnut dish in the form of a folded napkin in silver plate in 1873. It also made a tea service with gourd-shaped vessels in 1891. More recently Claude Lalanne has designed cutlery using naturalistic leaves for the handles.

Fruits and vegetables continue to be a subject for reproduction as these perish too quickly for permanent ornamental use. Everything from wax to clay to papier-mâché to plastic has been used to reproduce foodstuffs from apples to kumquats. A stream of milk can be caught forever pouring from a carton or a fork can twirl strands of spaghetti endlessly.

The permanence that illusionism offers can be used for educational reasons as well as entertainment. Because of the short life span of blossoms, the Botanical Museum at Harvard University had a collection of glass flowers created by a German father and son team, Leopold and Rudolph Blashka. Originally meant to be used for botanical studies, they maintain the beauty of their models forever. The elder glassworker felt his work "to be practically indestructible, except by force—so that, if we could come back in a thousand years, we would find form and color as today." Contemporary paperweight maker Paul Stankard encases his meticulously reproduced studies of wildflowers in glass, also preserving permanently the flower at the pinnacle of its life.

CONTEMPORARY PAPERWEIGHT MAKER PAUL STANKARD'S GOAL IS TO "CREATE BOTANICAL REALISM WITH GLASS." HE STUDIES WILDFLOWERS IN ORDER TO CAPTURE ETERNALLY THEIR TRANSIENT BEAUTY.

ALLUSIONISM: RE-CREATION

Illusionistic re-creation is the *re-creating* of an environment or the successful evocation of a nonauthentic ambience, that is one that does not originate with the current time or place. Both imitations and reproductions can be employed in re-creations, but authentic pieces can also be included in order to re-create what no longer exists. For the interior decorator, re-creation is an exuberant challenge.

Stage sets rely on illusionism to create the necessary atmosphere. It was stage settings that caused Plato to rail against the imitative arts, saying that "scene painting in its exploitation of this weakness of our nature (our inability to recognize illusions as distortions of reality) falls nothing short of witchcraft. ..." In most traditional theaters, the illusionistic scene created by set designers exists behind a

THIS SMALL DINING ROOM COULD NOT ACCOMMODATE AN ACTUAL STORAGE UNIT, BUT WITH BECKY FRANCO'S CHARMING TROMPE-L'OEIL FRENCH COUNTRY ARMOIRE, THE HOMEOWNER GETS THE DECORATIVE EFFECT WITHOUT LOSING ANY SPACE.

proscenium arch, which functions like the frame of a painting. The viewer is distanced from the stage and may not be able to see that the "marble" is quite broadly painted, more expressionistic than realistic; that the curtains are velveteen not velvet; or that the trees are artificial and the rocks made of Styrofoam.

But back in the real world much of the history of the fine and applied arts can be told in terms of revivals. Re-creation is the essence of revivalism. The truly new can be found only with the first appearances of civilization. Since then, with some notable exceptions—the Gothic, Art Nouveau, and Modernist (beginning with Art Deco)—every other style has been so heavily influenced by another period that it can be considered a development, a deterioration, or a revival. In fact, from the eighteenth century on, interior tastes have been defined primarily by a

RICHARD SHAW'S HOUSE OF CARDS APPEARS PRECARIOUSLY BALANCED ATOP TWO BOOKS. CLOSER INSPECTION REVEALS THAT THE STILL LIFE IS DE-CALED PORCELAIN, A MATERIAL MORE FRIABLE THAN PAPER; THE DANGER OF COLLAPSE IS NIL SINCE THE ELEMENTS ARE SECURELY ATTACHED.

A SCREEN CREATED BY MICHAEL GRAVES AP-PEARS TO BE DRAPED WITH FINE FABRIC—SUGGESTIVE OF A GRAND VIEW BEYOND THROUGH THE NARROW WINDOWS. SUCH A SCREEN CAN BOTH REDIVIDE AND ENLIVEN AN INTERIOR.

Fantasy scenarios can easily be conjured using only basic artist's equipment. Born of Brush has created an exotic atmosphere, complete with a leopard skin rug painted on the hallway floor, faux marbre on the walls, and crumbling Roman frescoes in the bedroom.

Contemporary artist Charles Goforth carries on the Renaissance tradition of painting collectors' cabinets. This technique allows individual expression while conserving space.

succession of revivals, with only a few moments devoted to truly new design. A nineteenth-century writer, Stephane Flachat, complained about an 1834 trade exhibition: "Where are the styles, where are the schools, where are the masters? Are we at the Greek, Roman, or Gothic phase? Are we adopting the style of the Renaissance, or of Louis XIV, or of Louis XV, or of the Empire?"

As we approach the end of the twentieth century, the taste for revivalism continues unabated. The voracious appetite of the consuming classes has been satiated by a banquet of courses representing every major, and many minor, historical styles, representing every decade of our own century. In the eighties this succession of revivals was so rapid that we almost expected an eighties revival before we entered the nineties. Chic interiors have been redone in Art Nouveau,

Art Deco, and the Modernism of the forties and fifties. Even the sixties and seventies have been "revived." "Antiques" shops now stock vintage linoleum from the twenties and thirties, kidney-shaped coffee tables from the fifties, bubbling lava lamps and plastic Tiffany lamps, which were, of course, reproductions from the sixties of the Art Nouveau originals, and cascading fiber-optic lamps from the seventies. Is it time for the eighties Post-Modernist fancies of Memphis to appear in "vintage" shops while they are still being copied by manufacturers of inexpensive furniture? They already show up at auctions.

It is somehow appropriate that the most durable style of the centuries has been based on classicism. The principles of design established by the Greeks and amplified by the Romans have influenced the Romanesque, Renaissance, Mannerist, Baroque and Ro-

Two details of the collector's cabinet shown on the previous page reveal much about the owner's interests. Family snapshots and books, left, as well as a tennis racket and theatrical mask, right, paint an intriguing personality profile. Artist Charles Goforth even depicted the family pet—which obligingly poses in typical feline fashion.

FOR PEOPLE WHO WISH TO DAYDREAM THAT THEY ARE IN AN EXOTIC LOCALE, AN IMAGINATIVE MURAL CAN BE JUST THE RIGHT ELEMENT IN THE HOME. CHRISTIAN THEE, A FORMER SET DESIGNER, OFFERS THIS TRANQUIL MEDITERRANEAN SETTING, WHERE FRENCH DOORS OPEN TO REVEAL A SEASCAPE BEYOND, ABOVE.

CREATING A FANTASY SETTING USING PAINTS ALONE, MASON NYE RENDERS BAS-RELIEF MOTIFS ON A WALL—MAKING THEM ALL THE MORE BELIEVABLE BY INCLUDING A WINDOW THAT FRAMES AN IDYLLIC BEACH SCENE, LEFT.

coco, Neoclassical (with its Etruscan, Directoire, Empire, and Federal variants), and Post-Modernist styles.

In most of these cases, the "revival" has been confined to applying the principles of classical design and sometimes only the details to what in actuality is an interpretation of the original.

The discovery of the petrified towns of Pompeii and Herculaneum in 1743 inspired the first wave of Neoclassicism, the first true, that is to say self-conscious, revival of classical style. The eighteenth-century British architect Robert Adam was instrumental in promoting this style. An archaeologist as well as an architect, Adam was very aware of the excavations in Italy and published a study of the palace of Diocletian at Spalato. He collected "antique cornices, friezes, figures, bas reliefs, vases, altars" and employed "painters, drawers, etc. to do the fountains, the buildings, the statues, and the things that are of use for drawing after and for giving hints to the imagination of us modern devils," as he wrote to his family. Adam took decorative motifs from Roman art—medallions, urns, vine scrolls, paterae, sphinxes, and tripods—and reproduced them in stucco for his interiors, arranging them sparely to create effects in the Roman manner.

DAVID FISCH HAS PAINTED A LIVING ROOM WITH A WIDE-ANGLE VIEW TO EXPAND THE VIEW, DISORIENTING VISITORS IN A PLAYFUL MANNER, RIGHT.

THE CASUAL QUALITY OF THIS SCENE, OPPOSITE, WAS CALCULATED BY TROMPLOY, INC. BY THE HAPHAZARD LOOK OF THE FABRIC DRAPED ON THE WINDOW AND THE SILVER PLATE LYING ON THE FLOOR, IT SEEMS AS THOUGH SOMEONE WILL RETURN TO RETRIEVE THEM AT ANY MOMENT.

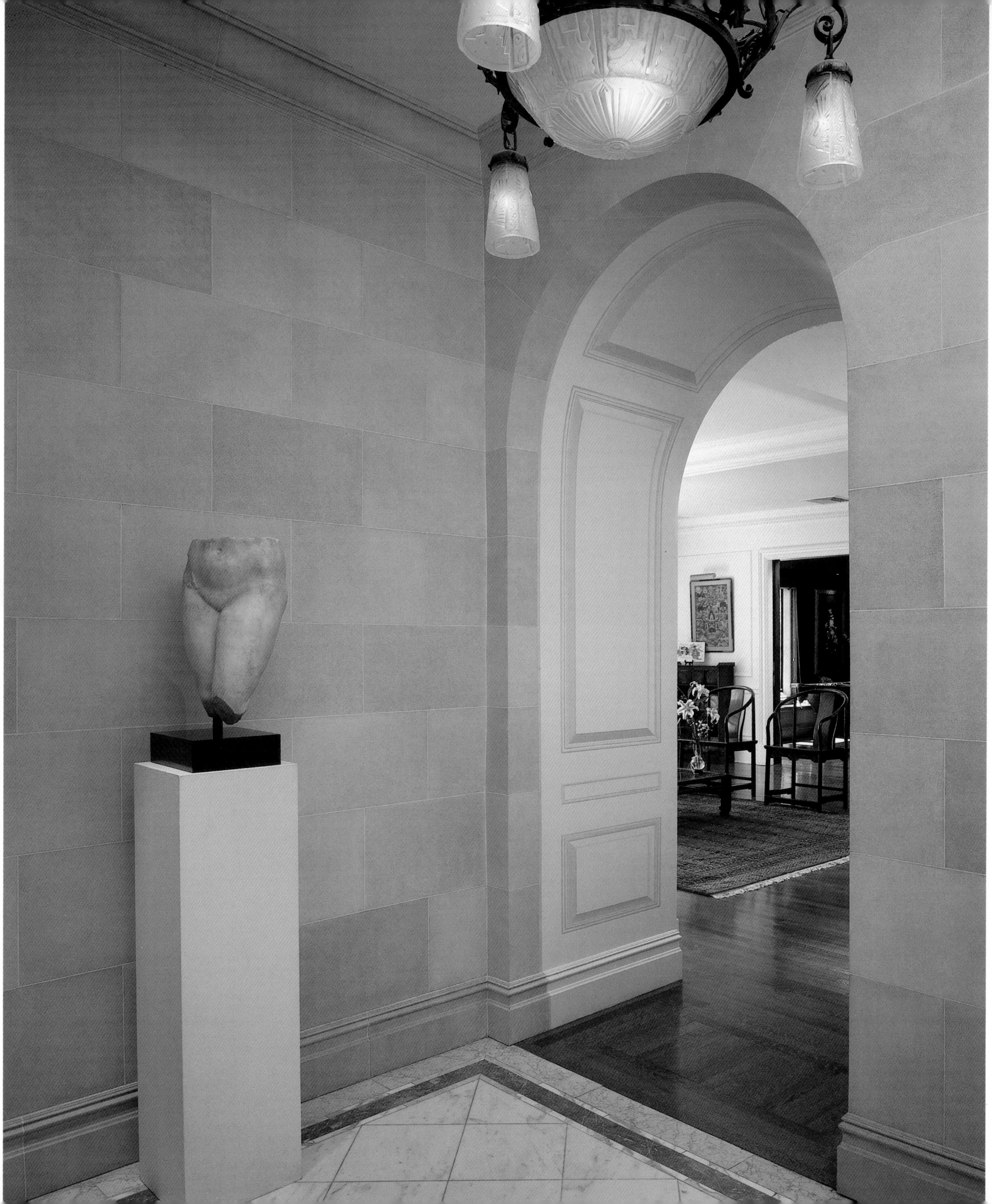

PAXWELL PAINTING STUDIOS'
FAUX MARBRE WALLS MAKE A
PERFECT BACKGROUND FOR
THIS CLASSICAL SCULPTURE,
LEFT. THE MOLDING DETAIL OF
THE ARCHED ENTRANCE IS
ALSO CREATED ILLUSION-
ISTICALLY AND ECHOES ACTUAL
WALL DETAILS IN THE ROOM
BEYOND.

GRAND SETTINGS CAN INSPIRE GRAND NO-
TIONS. JANE E. MILLETT HAS TURNED THIS
BATH INTO A ROOM THAT COULD HAVE BEEN IN
A GOTHIC CASTLE. THE FLOOR IS REAL STONE
AND THE BATHTUB MARBLE, BUT THE WALLS
ARE MERELY PAINTED.

Adam, although the leading exponent of Neoclassicism, was not alone in promoting the style. The ceramic manufacturer Josiah Wedgwood produced a line with Greek forms decorated by classical scenes in a cameo technique that imitated antique glass. Furniture makers such as Hepplewhite and Chippendale used Classical motifs such as swags, urns, ribands, and trophies. In France Charles Percier (1764–1838) and Pierre-Leonard Fontaine (1762–1853) popularized the Empire version of Neoclassicism, frequently reproducing first-century Roman designs wholesale. In England Henry Holland (1745–1806) simplified the Adam style, laying the foundation for the Regency, for which Thomas Hope (1769–1831) would become the foremost designer.

Contemporary artist Richard Haas was inspired by the Neoclassicists to transform a narrow atrium-like space in

THE J. PAUL GETTY MUSEUM IN MALIBU, CALI-
FORNIA, IS HOUSED IN A ROMAN-STYLE VILLA.
IT IS DECORATED WITH CONTEMPORARY MU-
RALS THAT RECALL PAINTINGS FOUND IN POM-
PEII AFTER ITS DESTRUCTION IN A.D. 79.

Peter Nelson's Canal Street loft in New York into a typical Neoclassical interior. Haas recalls that he was looking "for a solution here that would be light, delicate, ornate, and colorful. The lean delicacy of Robert Adam and Percier and Fontaine came to my attention at this time. There is a reserve and compression of form in these Neoclassical styles as well as a subtle color sense." For the Nelson loft, repeat patterns of Neoclassical details were silk-screened onto the walls and colors filled in. "Marble" floors were sheets of Masonite laid over a wooden floor. Views of the Aldobrandini Garden at Frascati and the Farnese Courtyard entrance opened up the space and were painted on canvas to make them movable.

Although Pompeii and Herculaneum were only provincial towns and perhaps not the purest examples of the Classical style, they have served as models for romantic re-cre-

ations since their discovery. The March 1797 issue of *Magazzino di mobili* outlined the decoration of a room based on artifacts found at Herculaneum. Percier and Fontaine designed a bedchamber based on Pompeii with wall paintings inspired by the Pompeiian frescoes and furniture. In 1839 Ludwig I reproduced a Pompeiian villa outside his Bavarian castle. Buckingham Palace also had a Pompeiian room in the Garden Pavilion, built in 1844. It featured a painted "marble" dado, plaster ceiling imitating stretched fabric, and a trompe-l'oeil landscape mural. The 1851 Crystal Palace exposition in London included a Pompeiian court. In 1860 Prince Jerome Napoleon moved into his Parisian "Maison Pompeiiene."

In the twentieth century Pompeii has continued to fascinate. In 1976 oil billionaire J. Paul Getty based his Malibu art museum on the model of a

Pompeiian villa. To achieve this his builders relied on a number of illusionistic techniques. The exterior walls combined real Italian tufa stone and cast concrete simulations. To decorate the walls of the garden peristyle, murals that were inspired by Pompeiian wall painting were painted, complete with trompe-l'oeil columns and plaster reliefs imitating stone masonry.

Pompeii in its preserved but destroyed state has been the inspiration for a number of contemporary re-creations. In Oliver Stone's 1987 film, *Wall Street*, when the ambitious Bud Fox reaches the height of his career built on insider knowledge, his upper East Side apartment is decorated by his equally opportunistic girlfriend in a manner that recalls Pompeii. In scenes from the movie, embossed plastic "bricks" were staple-gunned to the wall and bordered with a

PAINTER JANE E. MILLETT ADOPTS THE STYLE OF A ROMAN MURALIST IN THIS RENDITION OF A CLASSICAL FIGURE, LEFT. EVEN THE ILLUSION OF LARGE PATCHES MISSING ADDS TO THE BELIEVABILITY OF THE IMAGE OF A FRESCO IN DECAY.

IN THE FILM WALL STREET, STOCKBROKER BUD FOX'S APARTMENT HAS A POMPEIIAN THEME. THE DESIGN FEATURES A RUINED "FRESCO"—WITH PATCHES OF MOLDED PLASTIC BRICK REVEALED—AS WELL AS A FAUX MARBRE FLOOR.

layer of plaster and Greek key molding was drilled into the wall to make the point that it was all an affect, an illusion. Five layers of wall glazing, marbleized door frames, and an imitation Pompeiian fresco produced just the right ambience of doom for production designer Stephen Hendrikson. It took $200,000 to create this mock ruin.

Thomas Masaryk's Pompeiian room uses the famous town more for inspiration than for precise re-creation. Mosaic work, marble, stone reliefs are all rendered illusionistically in a luxurious contemporary bathroom. David Fisch's wall paintings are influenced by Pompeii and transform a featureless hallway into an event. A patch of sunlight streaming from a nonexistent skylight lends a perpetually cheery note to the hall. David Cohn adds an element of self-destruction to his Pompeiian-inspired mural by painting it over an un-

ANOTHER IMAGE FROM BUD FOX'S APARTMENT IN THE MOVIE WALL STREET REVEALS LAVISH NEOCLASSICAL MOTIFS INTERMINGLED WITH CONTEMPORARY FURNITURE.

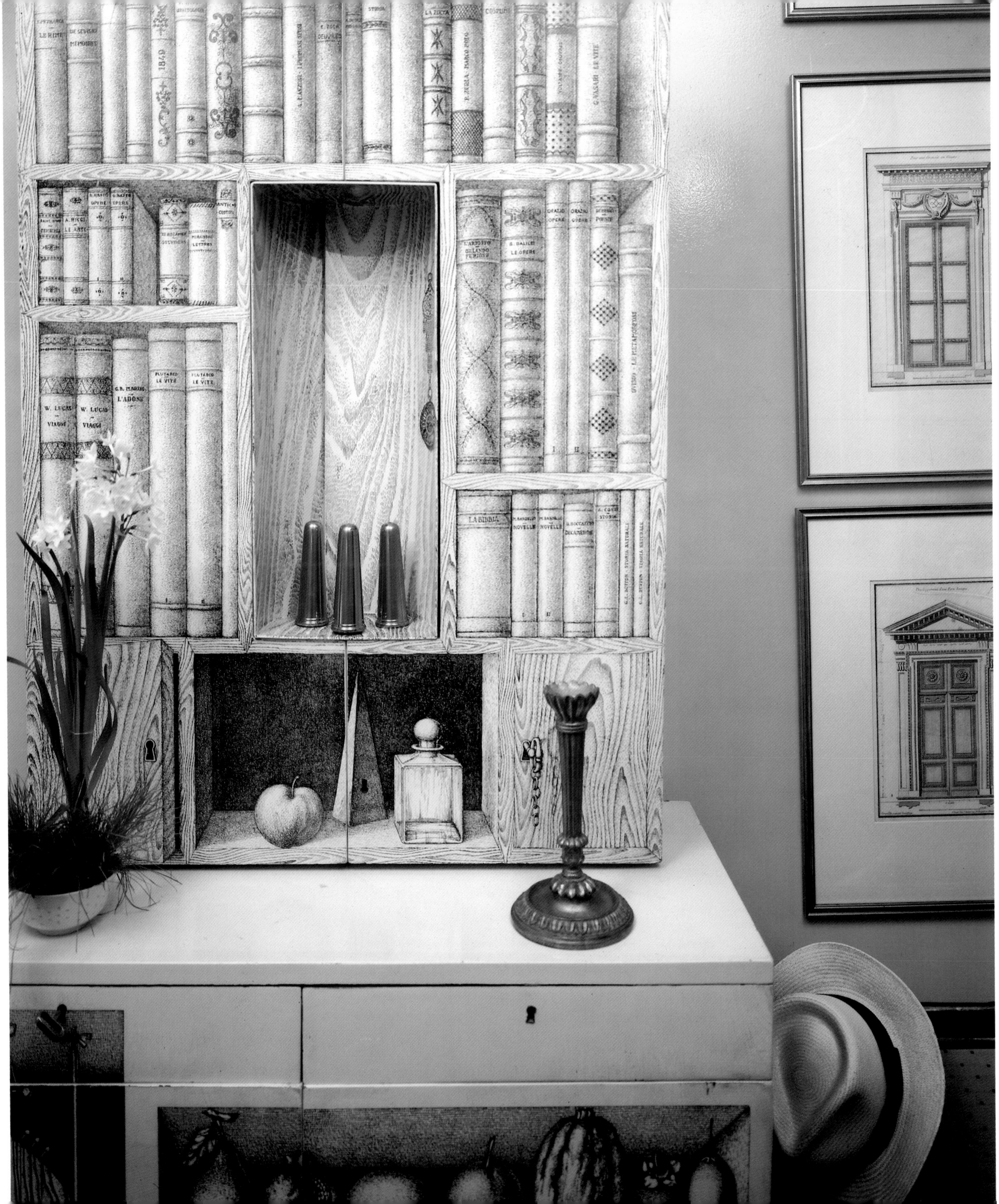
1849
L'ADONE
W. LUCAS VIAGGI
LA BIBBIA
NOVELLE
DECAMERONE

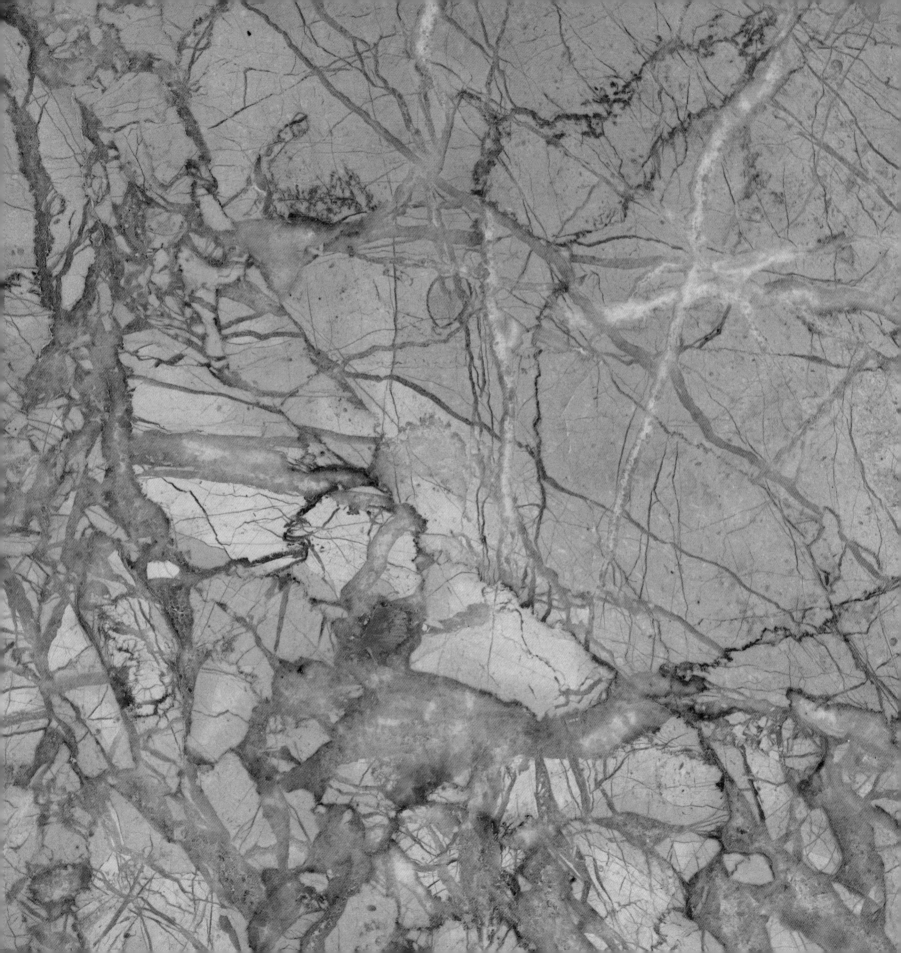

II

THE ECONOMIC IMPERATIVE

THOSE WHO YEARN FOR THE NEOCLASSICAL LOOK IN THE HOUSE NEEDN'T UNDERTAKE THE CONSTRUCTION AND EXPENSE OF NEW WOODWORK. F. SCHUMACHER AND CO. OFFERS WALLCOVERINGS THAT SIMULATE PILASTERS, MOLDINGS, AND OTHER ARCHITECTURAL FEATURES.

While these reasons do frequently overlap, one usually takes precedence. Economic factors have certainly been central to the development of many illusionary effects. The fine and applied arts do not flourish in a subsistence economy; fashion has always been dictated by the rich until quite recently when street styles began influencing high fashion.

The rich originally meant church or state, religious or secular powers. The Roman emperors built secular structures as well as magnificent temples to testify to their temporal power. Feudal kings constructed massive castles as fortresses and then decorated them richly, while the Catholic Church was building massive cathedrals. In Florence the Medici, princes, merchants, and bankers to all of Europe, helped create the intellectual flowering of the Renaissance, patronizing many of the same artists used by the Church, often under Medici popes. From the sixteenth century until the revolution in France, the French kings were the style setters of the Continent. With the rise of the Empire, Napoleon consciously assumed that role. He sought to revive the country's luxury trades such as porcelain and silk that had been greatly damaged by the elimination of their chief clients, the nobility. He encouraged the bourgeoisie, a class created more by the Industrial Revolution than by political revolutions, to adopt and adapt the style of his lavish redecorating schemes in the palaces of France at whatever level their budget would allow. Illusionistic, often mass-produced, substitutes, such as wallpaper for fabric, were used when the original was too dear.

Today, as then, it requires a certain amount of disposable income to begin to care how

PAINTED VELVET CURTAINS ENHANCE ROOMS WITH MEDIEVAL OR RENAISSANCE THEMES. HERE, JANE E. MILLETT'S DESIGNS—ORNAMENTED WITH HERALDIC MOTIFS—HANG ABOVE AUTHENTIC FORTUNY WALLPAPER.

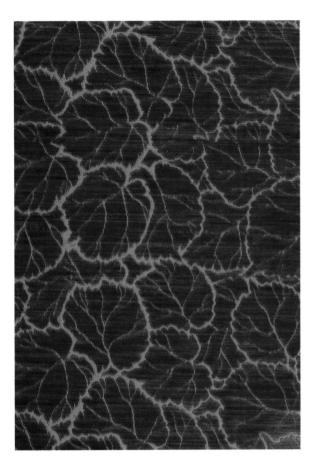

Brunschwig & Fils reproduces the elegance of a turn-of-the-century brocatelle in <u>Chantillon Cut Velvet</u>, but it is woven in bemberg and cotton instead of traditional silk. Its rich color and softness make it a sensuous furniture covering as well as a lavish drapery.

the necessities of life look. When all you can manage is a roof over your head, you cannot afford to be too concerned about how stylish it may be. But once basic needs are met, it is the human impulse to begin to embellish, often following the styles of the times, established by the upper classes, as closely as the pocketbook will allow. Copying the life style of the rich and famous may mean hanging a chromolithograph when an oil painting is too expensive or buying a Naugahyde lounger when a leather Eames chair is out of your price range. Flocked wallpapers, manufactured first in the seventeenth century, are still manufactured today and act as economical substitutes for velvet and brocade.

Textiles provide an excellent example of how economy inspires illusionism via trompe l'oeil and other techniques. In the Middle Ages heavy woven tapestries served both a practical and an aesthetic purpose: to insulate inadequately heated halls and to decorate. When not purely decorative, they were often narrative or didactic. In Early Christian churches they illustrated biblical stories and in homes of the nobility they recorded the family's exploits or told allegorical tales. Because of the nature of their production, tapestries are labor intensive and expensive. They require spinning wool and silk into yarn and dyeing the yarn before actual weaving can begin. Months can be required for particularly large or complicated designs. A perennial economical substitute has been canvas cloths painted to resemble woven wall hangings. Painted canvases that imitate woven tapestries are still being produced in French workshops and elsewhere. Jeff Greene of Evergreene Studios in Manhattan has designed a "tapestry" in acrylic on linen for Millie's

Place Restaurant on Long Island. Taking elements from the late Gothic fifteenth-century *Lady and the Unicorn Tapestries*, he presents them in a manner reminiscent of the nineteenth-century British artist and decorator William Morris, who had been much influenced by medieval style and craftsmanship. The Evergreene "tapestry" takes an original medieval source, filtered through a late nineteenth-century revival, and creates a new, multilayered example of illusionism.

Sometimes less costly manufacturing techniques or materials have been used to reproduce the effect of a more expensive fabric. By the late fifteenth century in Europe, there was a booming imitative textile industry. English artisans sold fancy "Italian" velvets that were merely homespun cloth flocked with wool fiber dust sifted onto an adhesive. They effectively and economically imitated the deep-cut pile

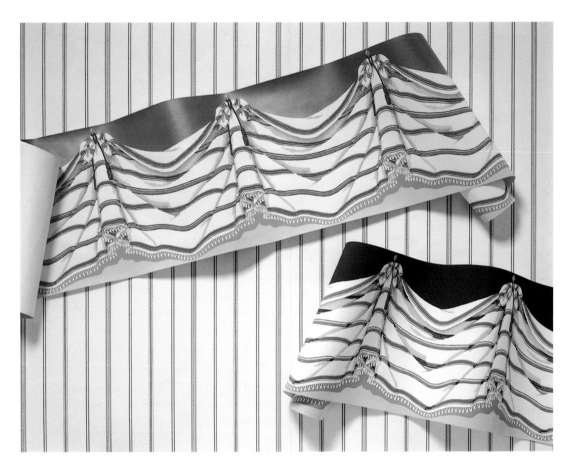

ASSEMBLING AND DISPLAYING
A LIBRARY OF CLASSICS
NEEDN'T BE A LIFETIME UNDER-
TAKING. BIBLIOTHÈQUE, A
WALLCOVERING OFFERED BY
BRUNSCHWIG & FILS, CREATES
AN INSTANT LIBRARY, LEFT.

THE TROMPE-L'OEIL SWAGGED
EFFECT OF THE DESPINA BOR-
DER, MANUFACTURED BY
BRUNSCHWIG & FILS, WAS IN-
SPIRED BY AN INSTALLATION
FOUND IN THE BENAKI MU-
SEUM IN ATHENS. IT IS PARTIC-
ULARLY AT HOME IN THE STUDY
OR LIVING ROOM, ABOVE.

of the expensive imports. Today the prestigious firm of
Brunschwig & Fils produces
designs of historical fabrics
but often by less labor intensive techniques. *Chatillon Cut
Velvet* re-creates in bemberg
and cotton a brocatelle, a brocade with a pattern in high re-
lief, designed at the turn of the
century. The Brunschwig catalog proclaims that it "looks exactly like the silk original and
is perfect whenever a look of
opulence is called for."

Fabric has also been imi-
tated by paper. Papermaking,
discovered by the Chinese in
A.D. 105, was not introduced to
Europe until the eleventh century. It did not reach England
until 1490 but the first wallpaper, intended to substitute
for fabric wall coverings, was
made there only nineteen years
later by a printer named Hugo
Goes. Goes then tried to imitate velvet and brocade that
were popular, and expensive,
wall coverings. A century later

ROBERT VENTURI STENCILLED

POSIES ON HIS WALLS TO SUG-

GEST WALLPAPER, ABOVE.

STENCILS BY ANDY HOLLAND,

RIGHT, ARE INSPIRED BY MOTIFS

OF COLONIAL AMERICA.

in England and France, using a cloth-making technique known since the Middle Ages, Venetian velvets and brocades were being simulated by flocked wallpapers. By the middle of the next century in Paris, in one of those ironic twists so common with illusionism, it even became fashionable to replace real textiles with these imported fakes.

Wallpaper could easily reproduce these two-dimensional effects, but in the nineteenth century, the challenge became greater. In the Empire period, a more luxurious mode of fabric wall treatments became stylish. Madame de Genlis in her memoirs writes that "fabric was pleated on the walls instead of being stretched, on the principle that the more material used, the more magnificent the effect."

For those who could not afford silk, illusionism was naturally called into play. The logical substitute for fabric was paper. Using woodblocks, the wallpaper industry began to produce trompe-l'oeil designs of draped wall coverings. Even though these early papers were still made in sheets that needed to be pasted together to make a continuous roll, they were nonetheless far less labor intensive than their models, which needed to be seamed, braids and fringes woven, and possibly hand-embroidered. One of the earliest of these wallpaper designs dates from 1808. Made by Dufour et Cie, it shows a white silk, striped in green, gathered horizontally and held in place with cords and tassels.

Of course, wallpaper is also fair game for the illusionist. When papers were too expensive to use, walls have been painted to imitate them. American Colonial and later Victorian artisans painted walls in patterns derived from wallpapers, often using stencilling techniques. An 1815 pattern,

also by Joseph Dufour, of blue-and-white-striped Roman shades inspired the contemporary trompe-l'oeil artist Sarah Janson to paint the walls of her bath in this design. Here, again, is an example of illusionism inspiring illusionism: draped fabric imitated by wallpaper and wallpaper imitated by paint. More recently Branson Coates, an English design firm, decorated a Japanese cafe in the mode of Greek Revival wallpapering by painting a continuous curtain of characteristic key motif trompe-l'oeil drapery over a dado.

Faux marbre effects have also been a common way to create a grand impression economically. Throughout the history of Western architecture the appearance of marble has been imitated in paint. The Greeks at Delos in the late third and early second century B.C. painted their walls to imitate marble. This practice was also followed by the Romans as

THE RICH EFFECT OF GATHERED FABRIC MAKES ANY INTERIOR SEEM MORE LAVISHLY DECORATED. THIS WALLPAPER BY CLARENCE HOUSE RECALLS PATTERNS MANUFACTURED IN NINETEENTH-CENTURY FRANCE.

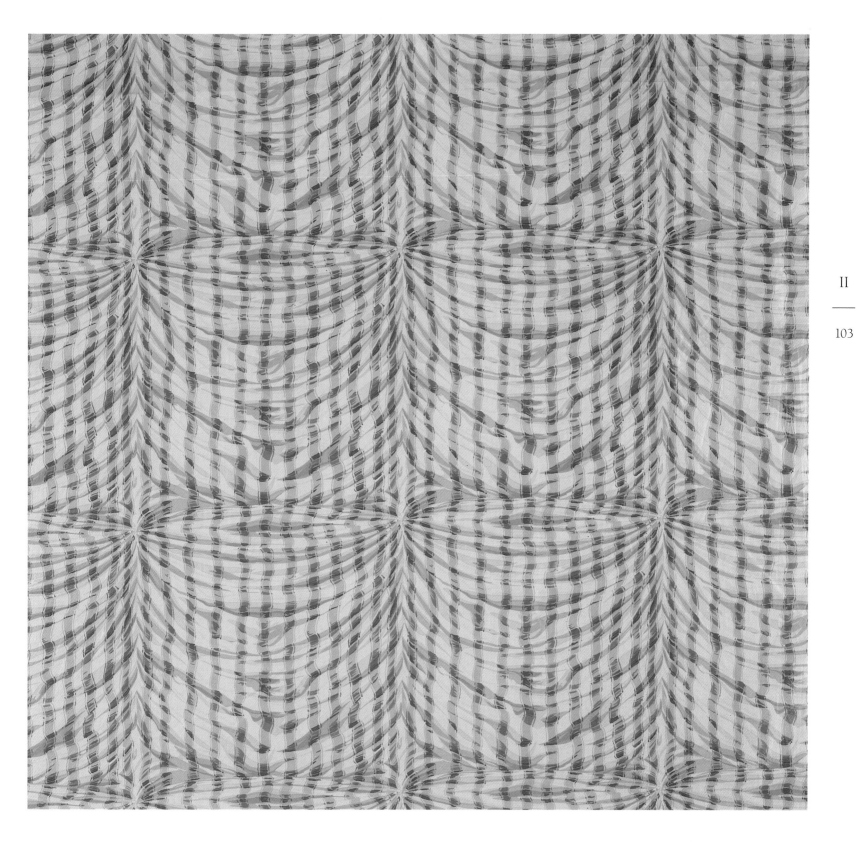

For the Metropole cafe in Tokyo, the British design firm of Branson Coastes created a neoclassical interior, above.

Gabrielle Bakker creates the look of aged stone illusionistically, right.

an economical way to reproduce the fashion of marble veneered walls, itself an economical illusionistic measure. From Pompeii and Herculaneum, which were preserved intact because of the devastating eruption of Vesuvius in A.D. 79, we know that walls were frequently painted to imitate marble in what has been identified as the First Style or incrustation style of Roman painting, dating from 200 to 60 B.C. Rare and exotic marbles, porphyry, basalt, vert antique, alabaster, and other stones were simulated in paint and arranged in decorative panels for both economy and entertainment. The eighteenth- century excavations at Pompeii and Herculaneum prompted a Neoclassical revival and popularized "marble" wallpapers in the nineteenth century although they had been used since the 1600s. The factors of economy and fashion again combined. Today

Brunschwig & Fils produces the Pompeii design, a printed cotton that simulates the look of Roman frescoes imitating marble. Contemporary trompe-l'oeil artist Richard Haas has re-created the interior of the eleventh-century Romanesque church of San Miniato in Florence with its green-and-white marble inlay patternings in paint for an apartment building lobby in Chicago. Although an environment of elegance is created with the faux marbre effects, the fact that Haas has chosen a sacred model for this very secular building makes the choice of model highly piquant.

THE RADIO CITY MUSIC HALL ART DECO COLLECTION BY F. SCHUMACHER AND CO. GLAMOURIZES THIS BATH. A FORMICA COLORCORE "MARBLE" TILE FLOOR ADDS TO THE DECO EFFECT, ABOVE.

FOR A LOBBY IN CHICAGO, RICHARD HAAS APPLIED A FAUX MARBRE FINISH TO RE-CREATE THE ELEGANT LOOK OF SAN MINIATO IN FLORENCE, RIGHT.

In seventeenth-century Europe real marble was used for public places only. In *Authentic Decor*, Peter Thornton writes, "Actual facing with marble was a form of wall-decoration reserved only for very special rooms indeed . . . its use was confined to adorning exceptionally splendid reception rooms, such as salons or very luxurious bathrooms." In all of the other rooms, however, marbleized woodwork stood in for the real thing in order to economize.

The same was true in America. Marble was not readily available, and marbleized as well as wood-grained woodwork was fashionable for both private and public use. The Marmion House parlor from a Virginian plantation house was wood-panelled around 1735–1770 and then painted (1770–1780) to simulate marble. Neoclassical motifs of urns and garlands decorate the panels between Ionic pilasters.

TROMPE-L'OEIL SWAGS WERE
COMMON MOTIFS OF DRAPERY
IN THE MID-NINETEENTH CEN-
TURY. THIS FABRIC, LEFT, IS IN
THAT TRADITION.

VICTORIAN GOTHIC—INSPIRED
FURNITURE DESERVES AN AP-
PROPRIATE BACKGROUND, LIKE
THIS TROMPE-L'OEIL STONE-
WORK WALLPAPER, ABOVE.

The effect was intended to be realistic and grand although the room itself is of relatively modest size.

Illusionism for economy is not confined to two dimensions. Period furniture and decorative objects are models for reproduction. Sometimes the ersatz must stand in for originals that no longer exist or are not readily available and are, therefore, prohibitively expensive. When a Gustav Stickley sideboard goes for $360,000 at auction, a reproduction from Alfred and Aminy Audi is clearly more affordable. They purchased the original Stickley factory in 1975 and prices for their thirty-piece collection based on Stickley designs range from $600 to $4,000.

There are numerous other companies that do a thriving business by reproducing period furniture styles. Victorian, Shaker, Colonial, French Country, and all the Louis styles, Mission, Spanish, and Southwestern as well as Modernist pieces designed by Mies van der Rohe, Charles and Ray Eames, Le Corbusier, and others are all available in reproduction. Shaker-style furniture can be acquired from a French company, Grange, or in kit form from Shaker Workshops. A real Doric column salvaged from a Neoclassical building could run as much as $5,000, but Ballard Designs offers plaster reproductions of classical architectural elements for between seventy-five and one hundred fifty dollars. The Museum of American Folk Art in New York has licensing arrangements with a number of manufacturers to reproduce items from its collections, including fabrics, wall coverings, bed linens, dinnerware, and housewares. The textile and wallpaper manufacturer Brunschwig & Fils produces numerous historical patterns. *Roses Pompon* reproduces a pa-

THOMAS MASARYK SKILLFULLY REPRODUCES
THE LOOK OF INLAID STONES WITH THE TRADI-
TIONAL PIETRE DURE METHOD, REVIVING A
NEARLY FORGOTTEN ART, ABOVE.

FABRIC IMPRINTED WITH CLASSICAL IMAGERY
CAN BE APPLIED TO WALLS AND USED AS UPHOL-
STERY AND DRAPERY WITH EQUAL APLOMB.
THIS DESIGN, LEFT, SIMULATES THE LOOK OF
CRUMBLING FRESCOES.

per originally manufactured by Zuber et Cie. in France in 1845–1850. Its *Hardwick Cotton and Linen Print* translates an embossed and moiréed wool moreen in the Winterthur Museum collection, made in England circa 1750–1800. This printed fabric offers the "look" of the antique at an affordable price. Whatever the style, chances are there is a manufacturer ready to supply it at a reasonable price.

But re-creating designs is not always a question of economy. Luigi Barzini in *The Italians* says that it sometimes proved even more expensive than the real thing. In the many cases in the seventeenth and eighteenth centuries where trompe-l'oeil mural paintings depict architectural features or sculpture the patron was rich enough to have had the simulated decoration executed in a three-dimensional form in marble, carved wood, or plaster.

Marie Antoinette's ministers protested the expense of decorating the Palace of Compiègne. In the Salle du Grand Couvert nothing was what it appeared to be; the marble pilasters, the onyx walls, and the wood doors were all simulated in paint. The large bas-relief and its smaller companion over doors were not carved in stone or modeled in terra-cotta but painted in grisaille by Piat Sauvage. It appears to have been fashionable to have painted copies executed after sculptured reliefs, not merely as substitutes since the plaster casts could easily have been made. It was the deception that was enjoyed. As Battersby says, "The attraction of illusionism was and still is its perverse substitution of the feigned for the real."

Equally ironically non-economical is the imitation of the rustic or the humble. In Japan at the beginning of the seventeenth century the military dictator Hideyoshi satisfied his taste for the rustic, a part of the tea ceremony aesthetic, by installing a country building in the garden of the Sambo-in in Kyoto. However, the interior of the building was lavishly decorated.

THE JACKSON HALL PATTERN BY BRUNSCHWIG & FILS IMITATES STONE WALLS IN EASY-TO-CARE-FOR VINYL WALLCOVERING AND IS AVAILABLE WITH A DECORATIVE BORDER, ABOVE.

A RUINED FRESCO RECALLS THE FALSE ARCHI-
TECTURAL DETAILING USED TWO THOUSAND
YEARS AGO IN POMPEII. THIS DESIGN, ABOVE,
WAS CREATED BY BORN OF BRUSH.

PRACTICAL MEASURES

There are also practical reasons for re-creating objects. Increased ease of cleaning has spurred the development of many substitutes. A vinyl "lace" tablecloth is more appropriate than an authentic one when the kids sit down for fish and chips. The hygienic virtues of substitutes have often been a common promotional ploy. In 1806 the architect John Nash persuaded a client to tear out "unhygienic" oak panelling and to replace it with wallpaper.

Linoleum was also originally promoted as a hygienic solution to unsanitary wood. It was invented in 1857 by Frederick Walton, who was searching for a way to fake leather by varnishing cloth. "Linoleum" resulted from spreading a mixture of flax oil, whose Latin name was adopted for the material, on burlap or canvas. Walton's li-

REAL MARBLE WAS COMPUTER-SCANNED TO CREATE THE PATTERN OF THIS VINYL MAR-BELESQUE FLOORING OFFERED BY CONGOLEUM. THE OPULENT FLOOR DICTATES THE ELEGANT DECOR OF THE ROOM.

noleum initially was considered a stone or wood substitute and imitated these materials.

This appeal to health continued as a major marketing tool in the 1920s when American rubber and linoleum makers advised housewives to eliminate wooden floors and woven rugs. In the 1920s large unglued squares of linoleum were advertised as "sanitary art rugs": "The patterns are the most artistic you can possibly imagine, ranging from neat tiles and wood-block designs for the kitchen and bath to richly-colored Oriental motifs for the dining and living rooms." The Congoleum company, which produced its movable linoleum "art rugs" in several Persian and Oriental patterns, gave young homeowners a chance to act progressively without rejecting their parents' taste for the finer things. They could have the luxury of "woven" rugs at an economical price with the

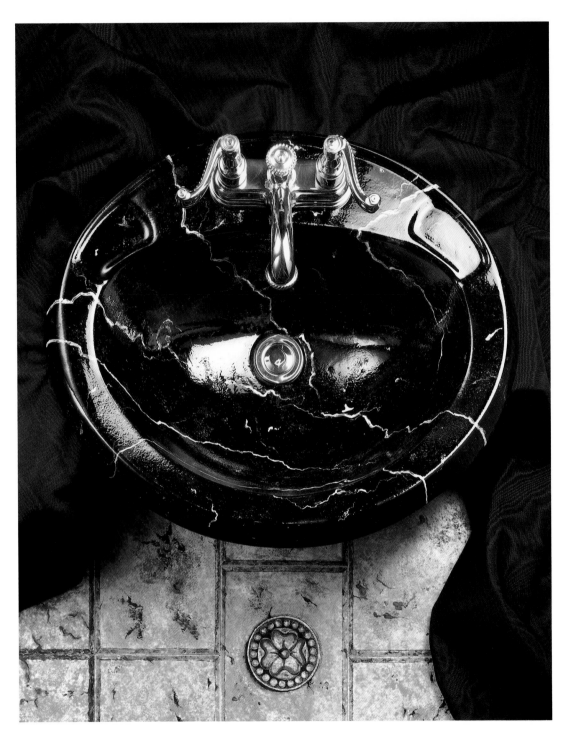

A SPECIAL TECHNIQUE IS USED TO GIVE THIS SINK BY CHRISTINE BELFOR DESIGN LTD. A LUXURIOUS FINISH.

A TERRACE WITH A FORMAL GARDEN BEYOND IS
ACTUALLY AN ILLUSIONARY EFFECT CREATED BY
DECORATIVE ARTS, LTD.

added benefit of easy cleaning.

Imitative "marbles" may actually perform better than real stone—yet another reason that faux materials are often substituted for the traditionals. The real thing is cold and absorbs body heat, is slippery when wet, chips and stains, is heavy, and is also difficult to work. Du Pont's "marble," Corian, was introduced twenty years ago as a simulation of white marble with integral, homogenous veining (meaning the illusion does not stop at the surface). It feels warm and resists staining, can be sawed and drilled like wood, and comes in simulated granite as well. In addition to Corian, an acrylic with a mineral filler, there are many other products on the market including Avonite, a blend of polyester, alloys, and fillers; Nevamar's Fountainhead, polyester and acrylic resins with fillers; and Formica's new polyester blend SURELL™, to satisfy the market. *Kitchen and*

Bath Design News says that about twenty-five percent of costly kitchen renovations and thirty-one percent of bath remodelings use these products. Corian and its competitors—imitators, if you will—are more expensive than tile or plastic laminate but cheaper than premium one-and-one-half inch granite, which costs seventy-five percent more.

Desire for greater malleability—at a cheaper cost—has motivated the use of imitative materials in interiors. In the mid-1700s when the French Rococo designers were still using wood carvers and stucco sculptors to decorate the panelling of elegant rooms, the English were using the cheaper and more easily worked papier-mâché, or "chew'd paper." Made of paper, glue, flour, chalk, and sand, papier-mâché could be molded into ornaments or pressed into blocks for sawing and sanding. It was cheaper than wood and

more easily glued into place than plaster. From the 1760s on, papier-mâché was commonly used to replace hand-molded or even precast plaster because of its economy and practicality.

Another more malleable eighteenth-century marble substitute was scagliola. Popularized by Robert Adam, the Neoclassical British architect, this imposter, a mixture of plaster of paris, pigments, marble and flint chips bound with glue, could be cast and polished. It was more workable than actual marble for complex inlay work or curvy architectural elements such as urns and balustrades.

The twentieth-century equivalent to scagliola, papier-mâché, and other castable compositions is polymer, which can be molded and painted. Focal Point, Inc., which has cast plastic moldings for Colonial Williamsburg and other restorations, prides

WHAT WAS FORMERLY A FEATURELESS ROOM WAS TRANSFORMED BY ZULEYKA BENITEZ INTO A FANTASTIC COMPENDIUM OF ARCHITECTURAL DETAILING. FAUX MARBRE COLUMNS, MASONRY WALLS, "CARVED" EGG AND DART MOLDING, AND A PERPETUALLY GLORIOUS SKY CREATE A GRAND SETTING.

itself on the imitative textures of its polymer—and its ability to replicate the look of age.

Today the artist F. B. Fogg casts classical columns, arches, and sculptures in handmade paper. Delicately tinted with pastel colors, Fogg's fragments add a nostalgic touch to a contemporary environment far more easily and economically than an authentic artifact would.

Metal has also been used to create columns, cornices, and other architectural details that were originally made in wood or plaster. Robert Adam cast pewter to resemble hand-carved wall ornaments. In the 1850s in America, factories turned out cast-iron facades and columns in imitation of Greek or Renaissance masonry for industrial buildings. Cast iron economically combined the intricate decorative effects of carved wood with the solidity of stone. Iron also provided relatively good fire resistance.

DESIGNED BY HAND-MADE PAPER ARTIST F.B. FOGG, EVERYTHING HERE IS CAST PAPER DESPITE ITS MORE SUBSTANTIAL APPEARANCE.

More recently hollow aluminum columns, fluted and painted to resemble their solid wood equivalents, which in turn imitated stone, never betray the illusion from a distance.

A PREVIOUSLY ORDINARY BATH METAMORPHOSED INTO A ROMAN FOLLY WITH FAUX MARBRE WALLS AND A BATHTUB THAT IS PATINATED TO LOOK LIKE ANCIENT BRONZE. BORN OF BRUSH CREATED THE SETTING USING PAINT TECHNIQUES.

THAT'S ENTERTAINMENT

Whatever the application or purpose, illusionism nearly always entertains as well. When we see an eighteenth-century soft-paste porcelain "cabbage" sprouting a spout to serve as a teapot, we smile since cabbages, as we know, do not normally hold tea. Contemporary ceramic artist Marilyn Levine's battered "leather" briefcase intrigues us far more than its actual leather model. Every blemish is carefully rendered in clay. Illusionism when used for its own sake, when not imitating reality for a purpose of economy or practicality, is always intended to entertain.

The queen of illusionistic devices—trompe-l'oeil painting—has amazed and entertained viewers for centuries. Pliny the Elder records the story of the competition between the painters Zeuxis and Parrhasius around 400 B.C. Zeuxis produced a painting of

EVEN THE MOST ORDINARY OF ROOMS CAN BE RECAST AS A GRAND SETTING. RICHARD HAAS FRAMED AN URBAN VIEW USING INTRICATE— YET PURELY ILLUSIONARY—ARCHITECTURAL DETAILING THAT EVEN EXTENDS TO THE RADIATORS.

grapes so realistic that birds came down to peck at them. However, he ceded victory to his rival when he realized that the curtain he asked to have drawn in order to see Parrhasius's work was in fact the painting itself.

The taste for trompe l'oeil seems to resurface during times of classical revivals—the Renaissance, Mannerist, Baroque, and Neoclassical periods. It also seems to appeal to those with an "enthusiasm for the bizarre" according to Battersby, and this is evidenced by its revival by the Surrealists.

Trompe-l'oeil painters over the centuries have delighted viewers with ultrarealistic displays of their own tools. A tour-de-force example is the cutout painting of an easel by Antonio Forbara. Painted in Avignon in 1686, it is similar to a slightly earlier composition by Cornelis Gysbrechts. In both works a palette hangs from a left-hand peg supporting the

THIS FIFTEENTH-CENTURY EXAMPLE OF INTARSIA, ABOVE, CREATES A VIGNETTE IN WOOD.

A THEATRICAL BACKDROP OF CLOUDS HIDES BACCHANALIAN NYMPHS, RIGHT.

ledge and the back of a painting fills the space under the easel. On Gysbrechts' easel is a copy of one of his own paintings—a conventional still life of fruit and shells with an ornate metal vessel.

Torn in Transit by the nineteenth-century American trompe-l'oeil painter John Haberle depicts the hazards of shipping artwork. A broadly painted landscape has been returned to the artist with the cardboard packing ripped away by careless handling. The canvas itself has escaped damage. The vivid red and yellow labels, one significantly asking for cash on delivery, emphasize the contrast between the torn covering and the mock painting—but all is painted.

The contemporary American artist Sylvia Plimack Mangold incorporates trompe-l'oeil elements in her compositions, playing them off against more obviously painted areas. Mangold's content concerns the

THIS SAUCE BOAT AND SOUP TUREEN IN THE
FORM OF EGGPLANTS BY FITZ & FLOYD ADD A
WHIMSICAL TOUCH TO ANY DINNER TABLE,
ABOVE. THEIR TROMPE-L'OEIL QUALITY COULD
BE HEIGHTENED BY INTERMINGLING THE SERV-
ING DISHES WITH ACTUAL VEGETABLES.

FOR A WINE CONNOISSEUR LIVING IN NEW
YORK, EVERGREENE STUDIOS TURNED A BLANK
KITCHEN WALL INTO A "WINDOW WITH A
VIEW," LEFT. A PARTIALLY OPENED "CUPBOARD"
REVEALS WINES, AND A GARLIC ROPE HANGS
PERMANENTLY ON THE WALL.

perception of reality. In the
early 1980s she began a series
of paintings of the moun-
tainous landscape outside her
upstate New York studio. The
scenes are painted impres-
sionistically and float on a
larger canvas, as though she in-
tends to cut them down for
later presentation. She borders
the composition with masking
tape to delineate the ultimate
size of the painting. The tape is

hyperrealistically painted,
confounding the most careful
viewer. Its superrealism contrasts with the loosely painted
landscape, carrying on the tradition of combining painting
styles with the aim of puzzling
and entertaining the viewer.

Trompe l'oeil also works and
entertains three-dimen-
sionally. From the sixteenth
century to the present, pottery
and porcelain factories have

Ceramic sculptor Marilyn Levine's Alle-
gheny Arsenal is an amazingly realistic
rendering of a well-worn leather briefcase. The plasticity of the clay makes it
an ideal medium to model into a representation of once pliable leather, now brit-
tle with age.

These "paper bags" are actually ceramic
vessels useful for storing and displaying
an infinite array of items.

produced convincing facsimiles of every known fruit and
vegetable from the humble ol-
ive to the originally more exotic rarities such as pineapples
and melons. In the eighteenth
century, dishes decorated in
stock patterns characteristic of
the maker were "apparently"
piled with courgettes, al-
monds, walnuts, hard-boiled
eggs, or radishes, also rendered in ceramic, carefully arranged and colored as though
real. These confections were
presumably placed among the
many side dishes, customary
at the time, as a practical joke.
The nineteenth-century workshop of the French ceramist
Charles-Jean Avisseau turned
out many of these amusing
dishes including platters that
crawled with all manner of living creatures. Avisseau was
carrying on the tradition perhaps best exemplified by the
Mannerist Bernard Palissy. Palissy designed gardens and
produced all types of ceramic

fancies for them: lizards, snakes, crabs, lobsters, snails, fish. His ideal garden was to have four grottoes, crawling with reptiles, and executed in *rocaille*. Palissy's terra-cotta ornaments crawling over moss-grown rocks were "enameled so closely from nature that live lizards and snakes would often come and admire them," according to the artist himself.

Trompe l'oeil may be instructive as well as entertaining. The remnants of a banquet were represented in mosaic in *The Unswept Dining Room*, a Roman pavement by the artist Heraclitus in the second century, which copies the third century B.C. original by Sosos of Pergamum. Lobster claws, fruit rinds, fish skeletons, wishbones, nuts, and other scraps from the table permanently litter the floor, each casting a shadow to create a considerable degree of illusionism. The messy floor reminds guests to be neater.

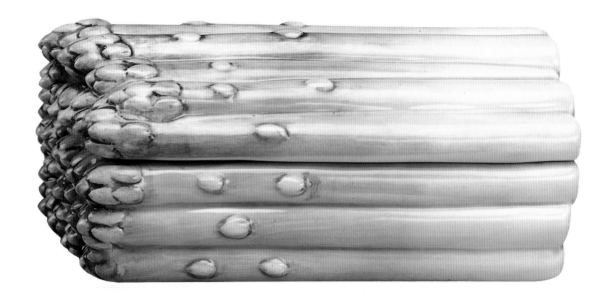

Since ancient times urban dwellers have sought a retreat in the country or at the shore. The roads to Frascati or Pompeii might not have been as clogged as the Long Island Expressway on a summer weekend when New Yorkers flee to the Hamptons, but many fortunate Romans did escape there. Sometimes nature's calmness has been created artificially in the city as when the early Egyptians painted their ceilings blue and decorated them with stars or birds in flight to suggest the edifice was actually open to the sky. The

AN ASPARAGUS BOX BY FITZ & FLOYD COULD HOLD ANYTHING, INCLUDING THE ACTUAL VEGETABLE AT THE DINING TABLE. THE GLAZED CERAMIC CONTAINER KEEPS THE VEGETABLE ALWAYS IN SEASON.

MICHAEL THORNTON-SMITH ADDED AN OPEN-AIR FEELING TO THIS DRUM-SHAPED SPACE WITH HIS PAINTED SKY SEEN THROUGH A TRELLIS-DOME. THE DEVICE HAS BEEN USED SINCE EGYPTIAN TIMES TO BRING THE OUTDOORS IN.

THE TROMPE-L'OEILISTS BECKY FRANCO AND
LEE AMES CREATED AN ELEGANT SETTING FOR
THIS DINING ROOM, DESIGNED BY GAIL AND
STEVE HUBERMAN. THE FAUX STONE WALLS
CREATE THE EFFECT OF A FORMAL DINING
CHAMBER.

murals of Pompeii with their illusionistic representations of vistas framed with architectural elements are another early example of this impulse.

The same concept was more elaborately executed in the sixteenth century in many villas. An outstanding example near Venice is the Villa Barbaro at Maser designed by Andrea Palladio, the leading architect of the time. The painter Paolo Veronese decorated the interior with trompe-l'oeil columns, pilasters, and niches with grisaille statuary and like the Romans, opened up the walls with painted landscapes. In the early nineteenth century French wallpaper manufacturers produced *Panoramiques*—scenic murals made up of small sections pasted together to form a continuous vista. *El Dorado*, originally manufactured by Jean Zuber in 1848–1849, depicted a glorious scene filled with exotic flora and fauna and with a few

Chinoiserie buildings thrown in for added romance.

For a rather cramped dining room, contemporary billboard painter and trompe-l'oeil artist Becky Franco with Lee Ames has painted the view of a grand formal garden seen through a columned arcade that is open to the sky. Scenic photographic murals also expand the space and delude the willing viewer that he is just a step away from the great outdoors.

Perhaps the rage for manmade grottoes with complicated waterworks best exemplifies this. Grottoes had been a feature of ancient classical gardens, so their use in this period, considered by many to be a continuation of the Renaissance, was appropriate. The interior of the grotto at the Villa Medici in Castello on the Lago Maggiore done around 1570 is encrusted with porous tufo, mother-of-pearl, shells, and pumice. The dripping forms suggest stalactites and

MASON NYE HINTS AT A GARDEN BEYOND THIS
VICTORIAN INTERIOR, ABOVE. THROUGH REAL
FRENCH DOORS, THE PAINTED-ON GREENERY
OF AN IMAGINARY PARK CAN BE GLIMPSED.

IN THE SAME ROOM DEPICTED ON PAGE 132, A
FORMAL PARK WITH NEATLY TRIMMED HEDGES
AND AN IMPRESSIVE FOUNTAIN PROVIDES AN
ENCHANTING VISTA FOR DINERS. A PAINTED
CORINTHIAN COLONNADE FRAMES THE SCENE.

yet they are clearly man-made. Gardens of this time had self-propelled automatons, with hydraulic organs that imitated the rustling of the breezes and mechanical fountains that sprinkled artificial rain.

In France in the eighteenth century, a ballroom was hidden in the woods surrounding the Château de Chantilly. Out of the real forest one stepped into an artificial glade with painted sky and woods. Painted cutouts of trees slid in front of the windows at night to shut out reality and a low fence some two feet from the walls left a space to be filled on festive occasions with carefully nurtured hothouse flowers completing the illusion of being in a romantic and idyllic setting worthy of Fragonard—an idealized version of the surrounding reality.

On a rooftop in Manhattan, James Alan Smith has less extravagantly painted a rustic wall behind a series of illu-

ALTHOUGH THIS ROOFTOP IS IN AN URBAN SETTING, IT EVOKES THE LOOK OF A RUSTIC COTTAGE WITH ITS FEATHERY PLANTS. JAMES ALLEN SMITH, WORKING WITH THE DESIGNER DAVID LAURANCE, CREATED THE EFFECT WITH PAINT.

sionistic terra-cotta pots filled with vining plants. This scene evokes a remembrance of sunny Italy. Karen Gunderson has made a career of painting skies. Her canvases re-create blue skies and clouds to re-mind urban dwellers of what exists outside their dark and closed interiors. Lillian Kennedy uses the same motif on her porcelain vessels, capturing a bit of nature.

Illusionism has satisfied many human needs stemming from economy, practicality, and entertainment throughout the ages. Occasionally it's even better than the real thing.

As we have already seen, these impetuses for falsification are rarely singular. The artist Richard Artschwager works with wood-grained Formica, a material commercially promoted for its economy and practicality. He has made it his signature material along with Celotex, a commercial paper composite product used for in-

A THREE-PANELLED SCREEN CREATES THE STRUCTURE FOR THIS "BAY WINDOW" DESIGNED BY CHRISTIAN THEE. PLACED IN A WINDOW-LESS LIBRARY IN A MANHATTAN APARTMENT, IT MAKES THE ROOM SEEM MORE COMMODIOUS.

expensive ceilings. Richard Armstrong wrote in the catalog accompanying Artschwager's retrospective at the Whitney Museum of American Art in 1988 that Artschwager's "chosen media, formica [sic] and celotex [sic], are unlikely carriers of meaning. But in his hands they are ennobled as art." Although trained as a painter, to earn a living Artschwager became a furniture maker, working with fine woods. Two events in 1960 inspired Artschwager to return to art making: a commission from the Catholic church to build altars for ships and seeing Mark di Suvero's first sculpture at the Green Gallery. Combining real wood and Formica "wood," Artschwager made a series of "wall objects—pseudo-paintings" in Armstrong's words. Since then Artschwager has continued to make sculptures using Formica, often in shapes that are exaggerated furniture forms.

Description of Table, 1964, is a rectangular cubic form covered with three types of Formica: A walnut grain describes a straight-legged table, a speckled white becomes the "tablecloth," and black indicates the void beneath the table. The sculpture represents a usable object and yet does not truly function as intended since its solid form precludes anyone actually sitting at the table. The use of the fake wood adds to the irony of the object.

In a similar but glitzier vein John Torreano has become known for his paintings and sculptures that utilize glass jewels. His gem-encrusted artworks reflect and refract light to create glittering surfaces. Most purchasers of these fake precious stones want to create the illusion of great wealth— and in limited amounts, this impression can be achieved. Torreano's use of literally hundreds of them in pavé-like treatments guarantees the

THE MARQUETRY PATTERN ON THESE FLOORS WAS ACTUALLY CREATED BY STAINING WOOD. A DELICATE BLUE FAUX MARBRE DESIGN ADORNS THE WALLS. ANDY HOLLAND CONCEIVED THE ILLUSIONARY ELEMENTS TO COMPLEMENT THE LAVISH DECOR.

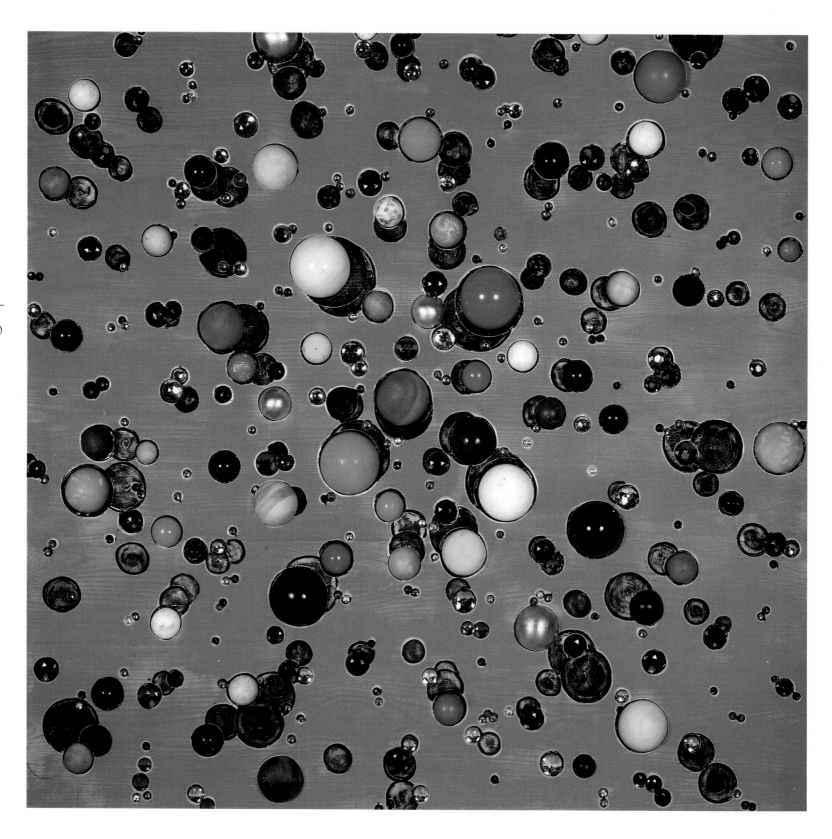

AT COLONIAL WILLIAMSBURG, ABOVE, THE
WALLS ARE GRAIN-PAINTED WOOD WITH A
DADO OF FAUX MARBRE. A PAINTED FABRIC
SWAG WITH TASSELS ALSO DECORATES THE
AREA AROUND THE CEILING.

JOHN TORREANO'S CLEVER ARRANGEMENT OF
WOODEN BALLS AND GLASS GEMS IN HIS 1989
PAINTING RUSH CONFUSES VIEWERS, MAKING
THEM WONDER WHAT IS COMING AND WHAT
IS GOING, LEFT.

viewer's awareness of their falsity. But the works are still truly beautiful. Whatever the impetus for illusionism, the results can range from the discretely deceptive to the flamboyantly false. It can alleviate a mother's concern over cleanliness when her toddler in his Scotch-Guarded polyester meets his match mud wrestling. It can enhance the image of an up-and-coming executive with a few well chosen copies of prestige items. It can transport us to another time and place when we visit a reconstructed Victorian town or go to the theater and movies. Illusionism can be cheaper, perform better, and maybe even amuse us in ways that reality cannot.

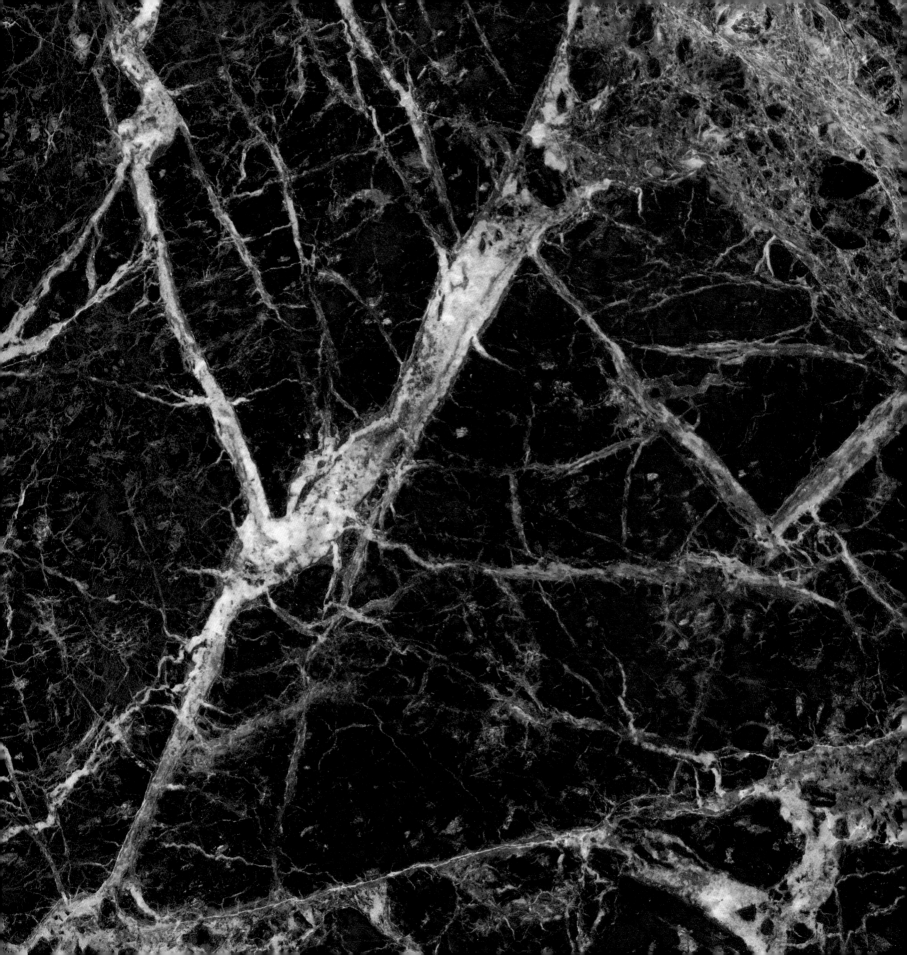

III

INSPIRATION AND APPLICATION

INTERIORS WITH ILLUSIONS OF GRANDEUR

A FEW CAREFULLY CHOSEN AND WELL-PLACED FURNISHINGS CAN COMPLETELY UPLIFT THE CHARACTER OF A ROOM. IN THIS SETTING, RALPH LAUREN'S HOME COLLECTION CREATES THE IMPRESSION OF "OLD MONEY."

"A man's home is his castle." We reign as kings and queens in our homes whatever we do outside them. Theoretically, at home we can create the environment that we desire. In reality this can only be done within economic and practical constraints; renovations and alterations cannot exceed the parameters of our lease or impact on the future saleability of our house, condo, or co-op. Incorporating trompe l'oeil and faux finishes allows us greater freedom to obtain the interiors we dream about.

Our surroundings are an extension of our personalities—real and imagined. As screenwriter and playwright Jane Anderson so succinctly states, "If your house doesn't mirror your own personality, what's the point?"

Home can be the stage setting for the roles we play in our lives. As a little girl, I longed for a bedroom done up in white and gilt "French Provincial," preferably with a canopy bed and lots of pink-and-white frills. It was my idea of a princess's bedroom and that was what I wanted to be, not the daughter of a middle-class family in southern Indiana. When I "designed" my fantasy bedroom, I was creating for myself a certain persona in the same way that Marie Antoinette did as a shepherdess in her "*petit hameau*" at Versailles. However, my parents, being sober and solid citizens, chose "Colonial American" in maple for my bedroom.

The same desire to create an extension of our *selves* in our interiors motivates us to tailor our offices to be a projection of our real or fantasy personalities. In the corporate world secretaries and low-level executives usually sit in contemporarily styled chairs at desks that are sleek and modern, chosen by the company's inte-

A LATE-TWENTIETH-CENTURY BEDROOM IS TRANSPORTED TO A GENTLER ERA, WHEN BEDS WERE CARVED BY MASTER CRAFTSMEN AND DRAPERY LINED AND SOFTENED THE WALLS. RALPH LAUREN'S THOROUGHBRED COLLECTION IMBUES THE ROOM WITH AN ARISTOCRATIC AIR, ABOVE.

WINDOWLESS OR CONFINING ROOMS CAN BE VISUALLY EXPANDED THROUGH TROMPE-L'OEIL PAINT TECHNIQUES. IN THIS CASE, ANDY HOLLAND CREATED AN ELEGANT LIBRARY COMPLETE WITH A VIEW IN A FORMERLY UNIMPRESSIVE SETTING, RIGHT.

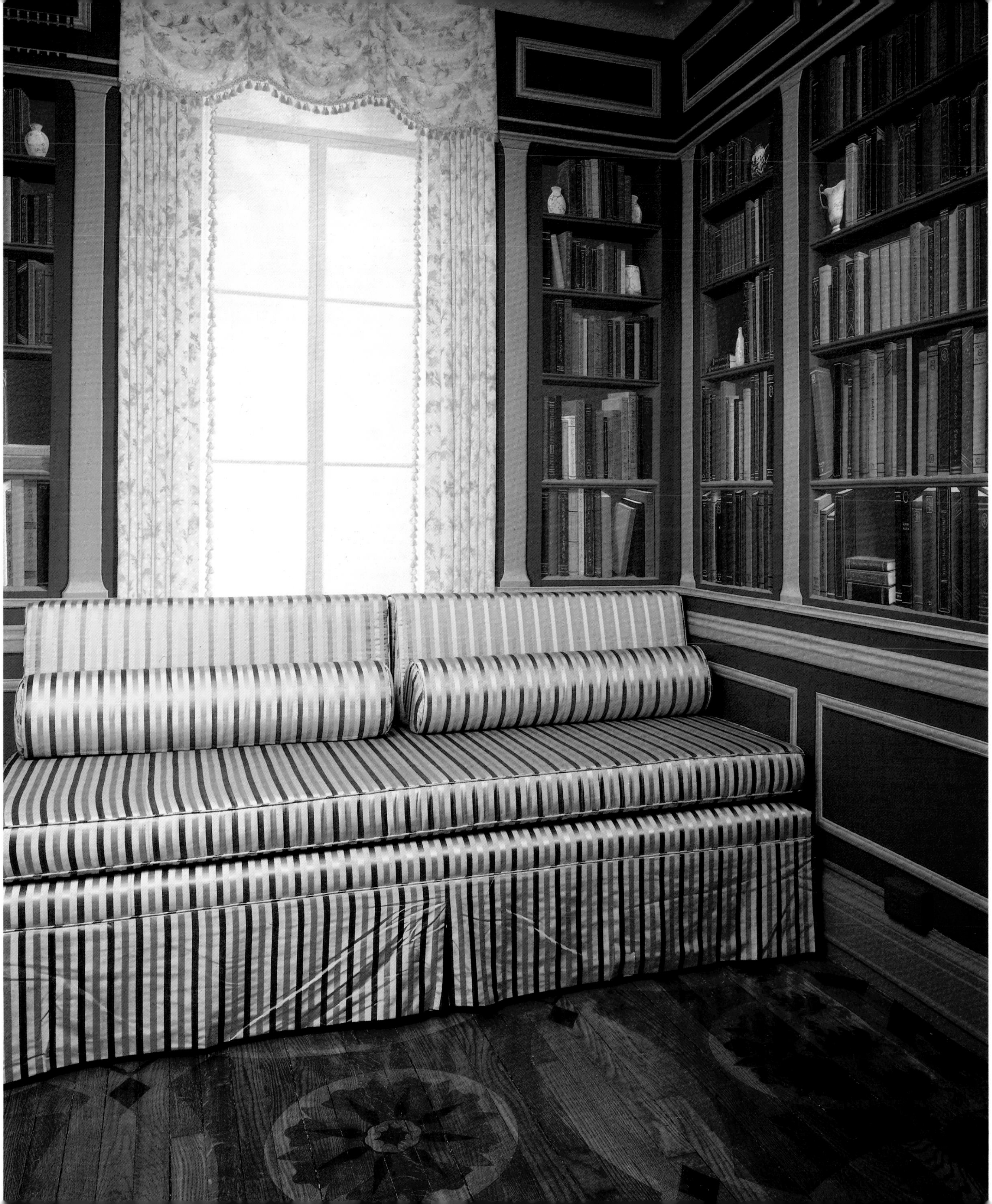

A DAZZLING ARRAY OF PAINT EFFECTS TRANS-
FORMS A MANHATTAN FOYER INTO A ROMAN
ATRIUM. TROMPLOY, INC. DECORATED THE
FLOOR WITH A "GOLDFISH POOL" AND BITS OF
CROCKERY AND CREATED THE LOOK OF STONE-
WORK, MALACHITE, AND MARBLE FROM THE
GROUND UP TO THE "SKY."

rior designer with an eye for efficiency and impersonal good taste. The higher-ups, however, surround themselves with symbols of power and elegance. Estée Lauder, head of the cosmetics giant, sits at a Louis XVI desk in an office that Witold Rybczynski, professor of architecture at McGill University in Montreal and author of *Home: A Short History of an Idea*, describes as being like a "small drawing room of a Loire château." Malcolm Forbes' office was a mahogany-panelled room taken from a nineteenth-century house, his desk a Georgian partner's. Again Rybczynski characterizes the office "as much a place for drinking a glass of port as for transacting business." These executives created an illusion that supported their vision of themselves and communicated that vision to all those who dealt with them—and were bringing the comfortable feeling of home to the office.

Every time we buy a piece of furniture, a lamp, a painting, print, or poster for our homes or offices, we take into consideration the image we wish to present to the world. By buying a Cricket Table by Lane, a replica of an early nineteenth-century table authenticated by the Museum of American Folk Art, we identify ourselves with the early English settlers of this brave new country. We can have the reproduction of Marie Antoinette's dressing table made by Grange if we prefer a royalist view of ourselves.

When we decide to paint, wallpaper, or renovate, we consider how others will perceive those changes in our surroundings and thus, how they will perceive us. Do we want to create a fairy-tale setting as I did as a child? Do we wish to align ourselves with the aristocracy or the revolutionaries made respectable by America's subsequent history? Are we hoping to emulate the latest trends? Illusionism can help us to create that persona. With the tools of illusionism—imitation, reproduction, and recreation—we can create the stage setting we want in a practical and economical manner.

Illusionism can occur in every room of the house and in every type of public space and has for millennia. From the wood-grained boxes of ancient Egypt to the Formica counters of kitchens in thousands of tract homes across the United States, illusionism has been at work—or at play. In every instance, illusionism has helped to create the setting perceived as appropriate for the activities of the space.

Every part of a room, from the floor to the ceiling, and every piece of furniture and accessory can contribute to the illusionistic whole. Starting from the ground up, floors have been covered with an infinite variety of woods and stones, aged bricks and glazed

CHARLES GOFORTH PAINTED A COLLECTION OF BASKETS ON A HIGH SHELF, ABOVE.

THESE JUSTINIAN AND PERSEPHONE WALLPAPERS, RIGHT, ARE INSPIRED BY HAGIA SOFIA.

VISITORS TO THIS MANHATTAN APARTMENT ARE OFTEN FOOLED BY THE ILLUSION OF A TORN PIECE OF PAPER LYING ON AN ELABORATELY PATTERNED FLOOR, LEFT. TROMPLOY, INC. CREATED THE VISUAL TRICK WITH PAINTS.

TROMPE-L'OEIL EFFECTS CAN BE GRAND OR PLAYFUL. A PAINTED FLOORCLOTH BY CHARLES GOFORTH IS "PULLED BACK" TO REVEAL LEAVES THAT WILL FOREVER ESCAPE THE HOUSEKEEPER'S BROOM, ABOVE.

ceramic tiles, leather and snakeskin, and even Oriental carpets—all illusionistically produced with paint (on the floor itself or on canvas), ceramic, rubber, and beginning in the nineteenth century with synthetics such as linoleum and later vinyl.

The forerunner of linoleum, painted floorcloths, popular in Europe and the United States from the 1720s on, have cunningly simulated stone as well as carpets. Most commonly they were simply patterned with squares or diamonds, but they could be much more elaborate. An advertisement in the *London Evening Post* of 29 January 1737 offered floorcloths of "the most beautiful Carpet Colours and other very curious Figures done to the greatest Perfection." Although painted floorcloths were quickly replaced by linoleum in the late 1800s, contemporary artists have revived them as a way to economically, amusingly, and

III

153

temporarily alter the surface of the floor.

Synthetics have provided a huge range of deceptive surfaces, from marble to used brick to wood, often with the added attraction of no waxing ever. Contemporary consumers can choose from pegged Mission oak, block ends, aged parquet, and rustic pine planks among other wood patterns reproduced in vinyl. GMT Floor Tile manufactures twenty different "woods" in natural colors plus eight "Designer Screen Woods" in pinks, blues, and grays that are unknown in real wood. Kentile offers *Olde Village*, *Saratoga*, *Federal*, and *Colonial* brick-patterned tiles plus *Rustic Clay*. The "marbles" available from Azrock's Architectural Collection of vinyl composition tile range from *Midnight* to *Dove White* and everything in between in color including *Cardinal* red, *Dresden* blue, and *Parsley* green. We can also have a

CHARLES GOFORTH'S PAINTED FLOORCLOTHS
REPRODUCE THE LOOK OF WELL-WORN
CERAMIC MOSAIC, LEFT. USING PAINTS ALONE,
GOFORTH SKILLFULLY CONTRASTS THE CEMENT
FOUNDATION, THE TILE, AND FALLEN GINKGO
LEAVES, ABOVE.

AN ESTATE PARLOR, LEFT, WAS PANELLED WITH WOOD AND LATER PAINTED TO SIMULATE MARBLE. THE FIREPLACE IS INDEED MARBLE, BUT THE WAINSCOTTING, COLUMNS, AND CORNICES ARE ALL FAUX.

A ROOM AT COLONIAL WILLIAMSBURG IS FILLED, APPROPRIATELY ENOUGH, WITH COLONIAL FURNITURE, ABOVE. THE WOODEN FLOOR RE-CREATES THE EFFECT OF FAUX MARBLING POPULAR IN THE 1600S.

"travertine" with a debossed surface pattern.

The walls of a room also can be illusionistically treated to create the effect of the cool richness of marble or the warmth of wood. Continuing a tradition that began with illusionistic wood-graining painting techniques (the Fourth Dynasty Egyptian tomb of Prince Merab was panelled with grain-painted wood), contemporary dens are panelled with fiberboard "woods" or plywood-backed veneers that appear from a distance to be real. Even less realistic are the wood-grained wallpapers. Brunschwig & Fils offers *Teawood*, based on the wood-graining of the Prince of Wales' seaside retreat at Brighton, and *Adirondack*, giving decorators the possibilities of papering a room to look like an exotic fancy or a rustic cabin.

Wallpaper has always been the great imposter. Designed originally to imitate fabric wallcoverings, wallpapers have illusionistically reproduced marble, stonework, brick, ceramic tile, and embossed leather, in addition to a whole range of textiles including silk brocades, rich velvets with flocking, meandering ribbons, and embroidery. Through trompe-l'oeil techniques, wallpapers have created the illusion of moiré surfaces, carved stone, and all types of draped and gathered fabric effects.

Although wallpaper was invented as an economical substitute for fabric wallcoverings, the imitator itself has often been imitated with paint. In Europe and Colonial America stencilling frequently was used to give the illusion of printed wallpapers. In the mid-eighteenth century in the colonies, craftsmen stencilled designs as simple as grapevines or maple leaves and as elaborate as stylish French wallpapers for the locals who

FLOWERY VICTORIAN CARPETS WERE FAVORITE MOTIFS OF NINETEENTH-CENTURY FLOOR-CLOTH PAINTERS. USING DRAMATIC COLOR CONTRASTS, CHARLES GOFORTH CONTINUES THIS VENERABLE TRADITION, ABOVE.

AN ORDINARY TONGUE-AND-GROOVE FLOOR WAS GARBED IN A LUXURIOUS INLAID PATTERN BY ARTIST ANDY HOLLAND, RIGHT. ON THE WALL, THE PATTERN INCORPORATES BOTANICAL MOTIFS AND A VIVID COLOR SCHEME.

THE MOST PRECIOUS OF WOODS, MAHOGANY IS EXPENSIVE AND DIFFICULT TO OBTAIN. ARTISTS PIERRE FINKELSTEIN AND CHRISTIAN HERBAUT RE-CREATED THIS LUXURY MATERIAL USING PAINTS IN A NEW YORK APARTMENT, LEFT.

THE FRENCH TRADITION OF TURNING ENTIRE ROOMS INTO SUMPTUOUS JEWEL BOX INTERIORS IS CARRIED ON ILLUSIONISTICALLY BY CARYL HALL AND DAVID COHN IN THIS BATHROOM DESIGNED BY DAVID BARRETT INC., ABOVE.

wished to emulate the fashion. Today how-to books explain the techniques and effects of stencilling for the enterprising do-it-yourselfer.

The architectural detailing of a room can be imitated in many materials as craftsmen have sought materials that can be more easily manipulated or mass produced. By the 1880s terra-cotta or clay was being used for stone details. Its fire resistance and its imitative versatility made it an attractive substitute.

Terra-cotta was used for both exteriors and interiors. In New York in the 1850s, the architect James Renwick ordered the ornate "carved stonework" of the interior vaults of Saint Patrick's Cathedral from a terra-cotta factory. In 1913 Cass Gilbert installed terra-cotta vaulting inside the lobby of the Woolworth Building, endowing it with a Gothic flavor. Similar grand effects were to be found in the townhouses of fashionable Astor Place and the opulent residences of the Upper East Side.

Ductile metal has also been used by the building trades to imitate other materials. Pewter was cast to resemble hand-carved ornaments by the Neoclassical architect Robert Adam. Stamped and painted tin looks like plasterwork or woodwork. Plated, it resembles hammered brass or copper-coffered ceilings, medallions, leafy crown moldings, and wainscotting. In 1909 the catalog of Missouri's W. F. Norman Company presented the High Art line of steel ceilings in Greek, Empire, Rococo, Colonial, Oriental, and Gothic styles as well as modern. When painted, the wall-to-wall coffered and patterned ceilings, moldings, cornices, side wall and wainscotting plates, and girder covers looked just like soft, period plasterwork for which there were few skilled craftsmen

available. (Lack of skilled labor frequently spurs the development of less demanding mediums to create an effect.) Today the company continues to produce stamped steel designs from the same factory and catalog.

Architectural details can also be "created" with trompe l'oeil. Masacco's Instant Trompe L'Oeil offers hand silk-screened columns with Ionic or Corinthian capitals, under window panels, and Neoclassical borders with egg-and-dart and festoon motifs all ready to be pasted down.

Interior illusionists are experts at entertaining deceptions, whether they are imaginary views or distortions of perspective. Sometimes through the judicious use of illusionary techniques, the actual architectural flaws of a room can be "corrected." Jocasta Innes, who has done much to popularize illusionistic decorating techniques

THE RUSTIC LOOK IS ACHIEVED WITH GREAT REFINEMENT WITH BRUNSCHWIG & FILS' ADIRONDACK WALLPAPER. ALTHOUGH THE WALLCOVERING IS OBVIOUSLY A SHAM, ITS DELIBERATELY UNCONVINCING QUALITY ADDS A HUMOROUS TOUCH TO THE ROOM.

III
———
162

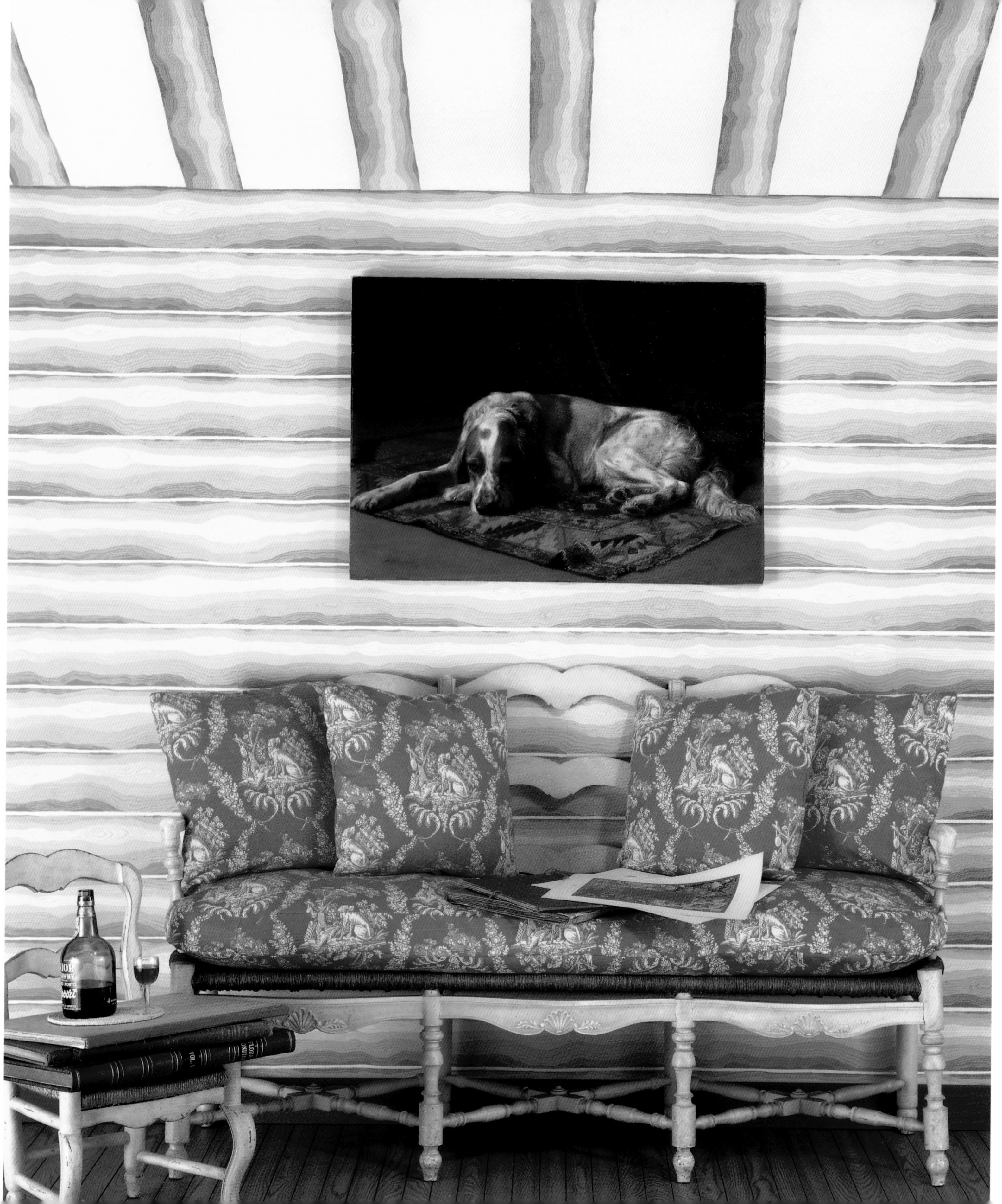

through her how-to books, has written: "Not many people are lucky enough to live in classically-proportioned rooms, but there is a lot that can be done to rectify awkward spaces, restore harmony, and introduce 'firmness.'"

Innes goes on to describe how paint techniques can transform a room—a painted line can mimic a dado, a stencilled frieze can create the illusion of a cornice.

There are other, even more elaborate possibilities to consider. A "window" with an extraordinary view can replace the brick wall of the neighboring building, providing a fantasy vista. Ceilings can be lifted by turning them into expansive blue skies. Grand architecture can be conjured up through the trompe l'oeilist's wizardry, a bit of paint on a flat wall becoming a Baroque extravaganza. Or the artist can bewilder the viewer by altering what is expected: The real can

THE FLORAL WALLPAPER SHOWN HERE IS REAL, BUT THE CARPETING THAT COMPLEMENTS IT WAS PAINTED BY ARTIST ANDY HOLLAND, ABOVE. THIS TROMPE-L'OEIL EFFECT WAS NOT ONLY ECONOMICAL BUT ALSO A MEANS OF MATCHING WALL AND FLOOR MOTIFS, RIGHT.

BANNERS AND BUNTING ARE MATERIALS OF THE MOMENT, NOT INTENDED TO OUTLAST THE CELEBRATION. BUT THE TROMPE-L'OEIL PAINTER CAN PROLONG THEIR LIVES INDEFINITELY. CREATING A HERALDIC SETTING, SCOTT WATERMAN HAS ADDED FLAGS, BANNERS, AND GRAPE BOUGHS OVER WINDOWS THAT OPEN ONTO "VIEWS" OF OVERGROWN GARDENS, ABOVE.

THE HOMEOWNER NEED NO LONGER BE CONDEMNED TO LIVING IN BLAND, FEATURELESS ROOMS. CLARENCE HOUSE OFFERS A FULL LINE OF WALLPAPER BORDERS THAT REALISTICALLY IMITATE THREE-DIMENSIONAL ARCHITECTURAL DETAILING, LEFT.

be painted over in a pattern that is at odds with it, making corners appear or disappear.

Sometimes the shell of the room is totally transformed. We have already seen how trompe-l'oeil painting can create illusions of grandeur in two dimensions. It also happens in three. Fashionable rooms in nineteenth-century France were draped and roped with hundreds of yards of fabric to evoke the romance of tents pitched in exotic locales. A domestic setting could be transformed into a scene of adventure—a Moorish garden pavilion, a sheik's desert home, or even Napoleon's camp on enemy turf. Today, the effect is just as intriguing, and many enterprising designers are transforming rooms by tenting ceilings, draping ordinary furniture with lavish fabric, and "fabricating" walls by applying textiles with appealing textures and patterns.

Draped effects were often

imitated in plaster. In the early 1800s the English architect Sir John Soane illusionistically "tented" two small rooms using shallow plaster domes carved to resemble taut fabric. In his London house he stretched what he called a "rich canopy" over his small breakfast parlor and repeated this conceit in his country house, Pitzhanger Manor. More recently the French designer Jean-Louis Riccardi used this same technique to create a luxurious Parisian dining room—an illustration of how we can draw on the past to innovate in the present.

One of the advantages of creating visual illusions is the permanent effect that they create. Illusionism offers flowers that are constantly in bloom, trompe-l'oeil larders that are always filled with plenty of the freshest fruits and vegetables, and perpetually sunny skies or starry nights.

This illusionistic perma-

PERCHED ON A GOTHIC PARAPET, THIS MENACING GARGOYLE, ABOVE, IS ONLY A PAINTED GRISAILLE IMAGE, CREATED BY ENRI AND GIL. THE ILLUSION IS PARTICULARLY AUTHENTIC BECAUSE IT IS PAINTED WHERE TWO WALLS MEET, CAUSING THE MONSTER TO LOOM FORWARD. AT THE SAME TIME, THE EFFECT VISUALLY FLATTENS THE REAL ARCHITECTURE.

IN AN ENTRY HALL, DEEPLY TUFTED RICH RED
FABRIC AND WOODEN WAINSCOTTING CREATE A
DIGNIFIED FIRST IMPRESSION, ABOVE. ON SEC-
OND GLANCE, THE VISITOR REALIZES THAT THE
MATERIALS ARE ACTUALLY PAINTED SURFACES.
CREATED BY ARTIST SCOTT WATERMAN, THESE
EFFECTS WERE INSPIRED BY A LONGSTANDING
TRADITION OF SIMULATING TEXTILES TO GIVE
ROOMS A RICH LOOK.

nence is another way we take control of our environment, exercising our "royal" prerogative over our surroundings. Everyone knows we have no power over the weather, but through illusionism, we can attempt it. Nature is fickle, constantly changing, fair one moment, foul the next. With the illusionist's art, we can control this force. The Egyptians did this in their temples, and countless other examples exist throughout history. Sometimes the effects are quite grand as they were in Baroque cathedrals. At other times, they are more modest as when Decorative Arts, Ltd., painted a blue sky ceiling for a small kitchen.

Sky ceilings are just one way for us to introduce nature indoors. Sometimes it is even more subtle. Mrs. Paul Mellon has "her floors painted with shadows, so that on a dreary day the sunlight still seems to be streaming in," according to John Fairchild in *Chic Savages*.

A GRACEFUL CEILING TREATMENT CAN COMPLETELY CHANGE AND UPLIFT THE CHARACTER OF A ROOM. IN THIS ROOM DECORATED BY DAVID BARRETT, ABOVE, GATHERED FABRIC APPEARS TO BILLOW OVERHEAD, BUT IS ACTUALLY A CONVINCING PAINTED EFFECT CREATED BY ARTIST DAVID COHN.

THE REFRIGERATOR DOOR HAS BEEN PAINTED TO MATCH THE CEDAR WALLS OF THIS KITCHEN. THE WOOD GRAINING BY RICHARD LOWELL NEAS SUCCESSFULLY CAMOUFLAGES THIS MODERN DAY CONVENIENCE, RIGHT.

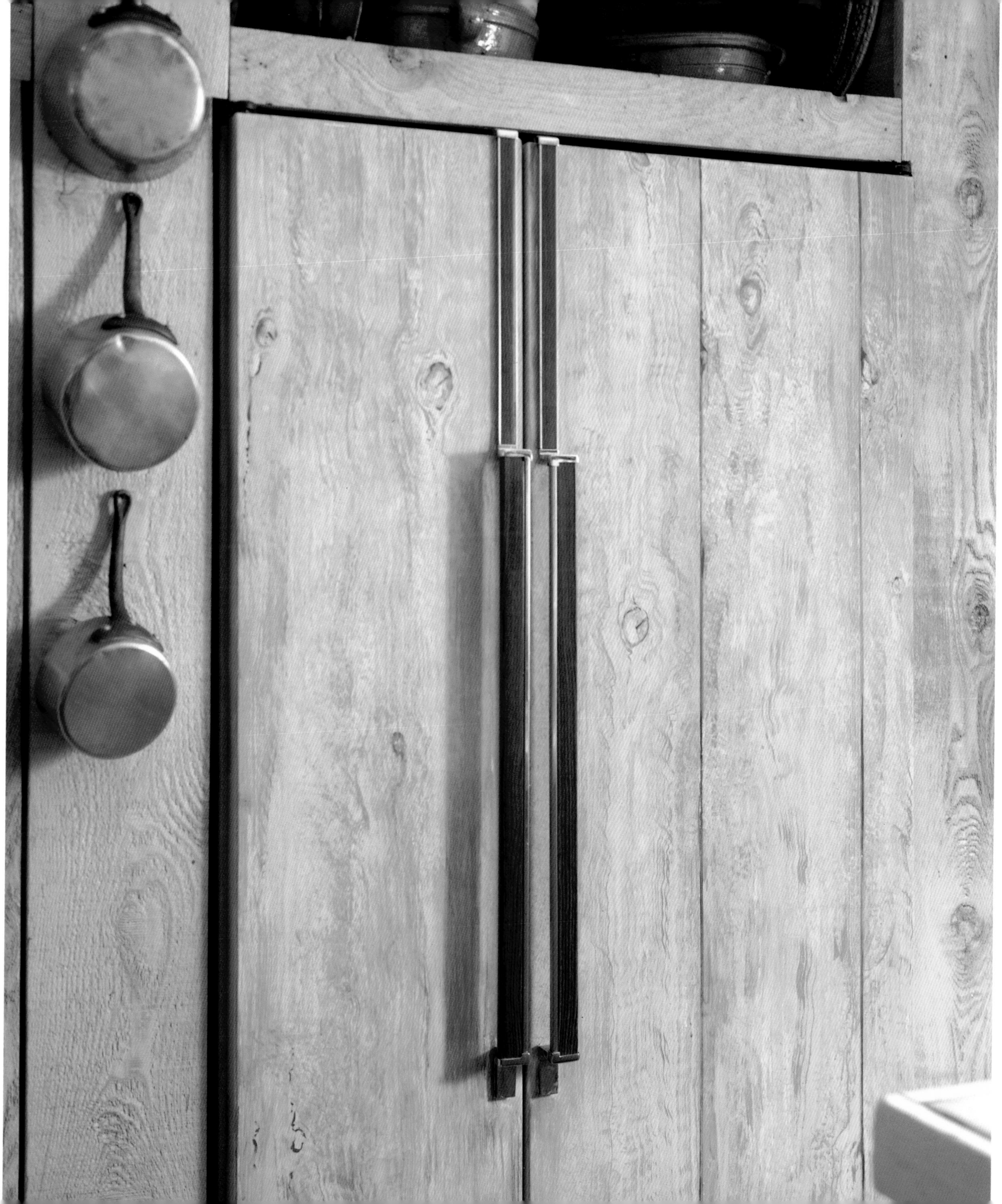

IN THE SPIRIT OF AN AMUSE-
MENT PARK FUNHOUSE, DAVID
BALL AND MEGAN PARRY PLAY
PERCEPTION TRICKS BY EXTEND-
ING THE RED-CARPETED FLOOR
ONTO THE WALL WITH PAINT.

The views from our windows can also be altered or even created with false windows and illusionistic perspectives. Whether the vista is the Veneto, as it is from the sixteenth-century Villa Barbaro at Maser or the Chicago skyline, illusionists have sought to improve on it. Paolo Veronese embellished the Palladian rooms in Maser with a dado of "marble," statuary in false niches, Ionic columns, and a romanticized landscape far more eventful than the placid plains actually seen from the windows. In present-day Chicago trompe-l'oeil artist Richard Haas has painted an equally idealized view, but this time it is of modern skyscrapers. Again, the view, painted on sliding panels, is similar to the actual one but somewhat more interesting. Also like Veronese, Haas has enhanced the architecture of the setting by adding a wide terrace.

The grand illusion of re-cre-

TO ENLARGE A COMPACT VICTORIAN-STYLE OFFICE, MASON NYE PAINTED A RESTFUL PARK SCENE ON THE WALL. THE ILLUSION IS HEIGHTENED BY THE ADDITION OF REAL FRENCH DOORS TO FRAME THE SCENE.

ation occurs when all parts of an interior are contrived to evoke another time or place. With thousands of years of history and art to draw on, illusionists have endless sources. A walk through almost any furniture store confirms the availability of furniture designed to reproduce a Biedermeier study, an Elizabethan dining room, a Louis XIV bedroom, or, at least, someone's interpretation of them.

Often these reproductions come with the seal of approval from well-respected institutions. Colonial Williamsburg offers thousands of items including furniture, fabrics, pewter, brass, and china. Victorian Collectibles reproduces an extensive selection of the wallpaper from the Brillion Collection owned by the Cooper-Hewitt Museum, New York; Schumacher makes fabrics chosen from the Abby Aldrich Rockefeller Folk Art Collections; Brunschwig & Fils

DECORATIVE ARTS, LTD. OF HOUSTON "MOVED" THIS ROOM OUTDOORS, ABOVE. THE CORNICE IS REAL, BUT THE LEDGES AND LATTICEWORK ARE NOT. BOTH THE ACTUAL AND THE FALSE ARCHITECTURE ARE COVERED BY A ROSE BUSH.

THE SHELVES OF THIS CUPBOARD PAINTED BY RICHARD LOWELL NEAS WILL ALWAYS BE FILLED WITH FRESH FRUITS, VEGETABLES, AND HOMEMADE PRESERVES, RIGHT. THE LARGE SACK OF GRAIN, WHILE A PLAUSIBLE PART OF A RUSTIC SCENE SUGGESTED HERE, IS HIGHLY UNLIKELY TO BE FOUND IN A CONTEMPORARY KITCHEN. BY PAINTING IT, THE ARTIST ADDS TO THE ILLUSION OF AN OLD-FASHIONED PANTRY.

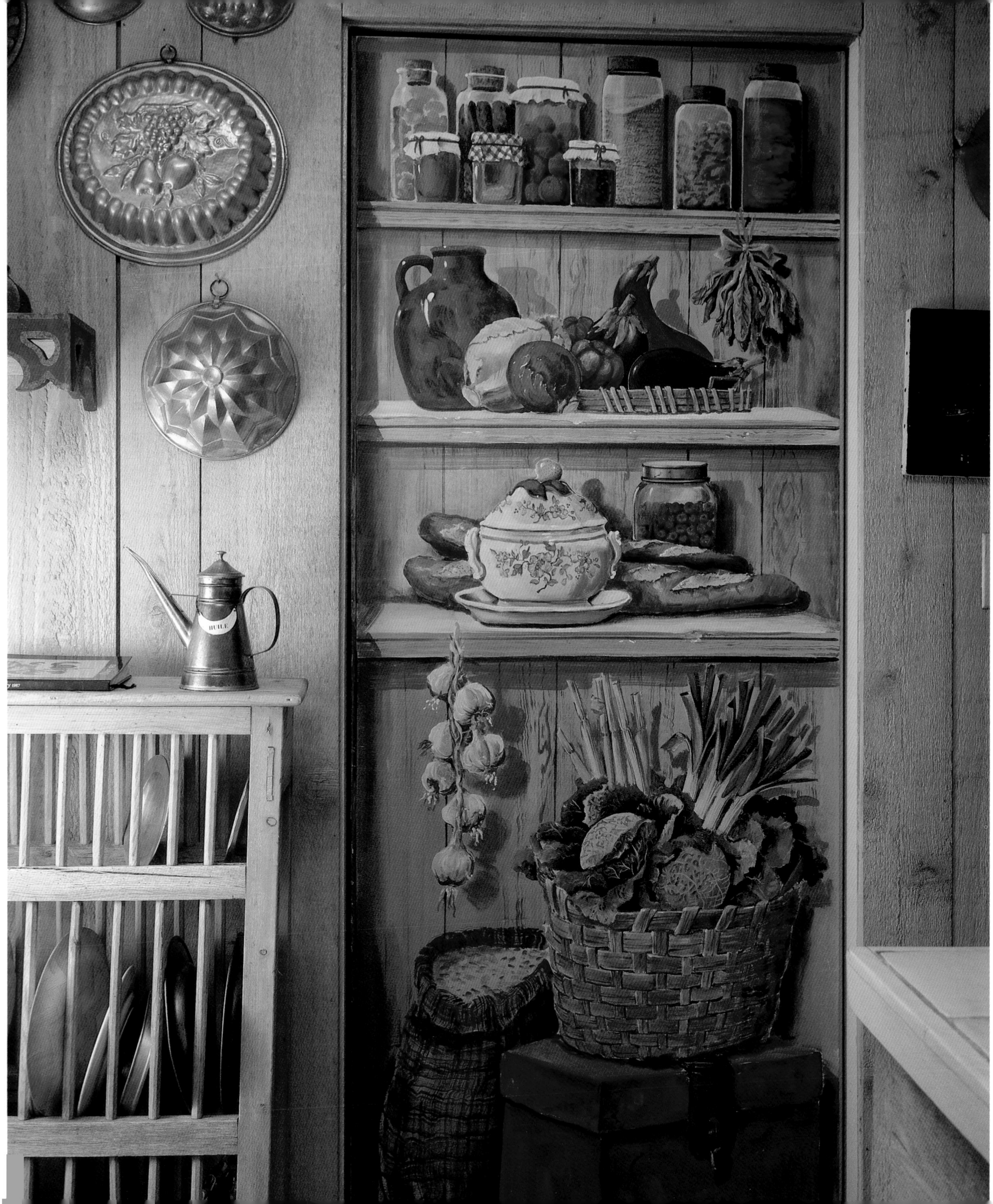
HUILE

has copied wallpapers and textiles from the Winterthur Museum, the Musée des Arts Décoratifs in Paris, the Benaki Museum in Athens, and others; and C & A Wallcoverings has a collection of replica wallpapers from the Victoria and Albert Museum in London. The Museum of American Folk Art has licensed Lane Furniture to make a line based on their collection including an open armchair used by Martha Washington at Mt. Vernon. Using any of these pieces in period interiors becomes even more exciting when combined with stencils and other applied techniques that simulate architectural flourishes.

Baker Furniture has manufactured a line chosen by the New York design firm McMillen. McMillen's president, Betty Sherrill, says that "it has been a dream of McMillen's to do a collection for people who couldn't afford costly antiques but did want

A FRENCH BLOCK-PRINTED WALLPAPER DATING FROM CIRCA 1825 AND FOUND IN THE SAMUEL FOWLER HOUSE OF SALEM, MASSACHUSETTS, WAS THE MODEL FOR THIS CONTEMPORARY REPRODUCTION BY BRUNSCHWIG & FILS.

This Regency dwarf breakfront is actually a reproduction, but is convincing enough to add an aristocratic air to the dining room. The piece was copied by the Baker Furniture Company from the Duke of Wellington's home.

beautiful things." This collection includes an eighteenth-century Venetian red lacquer secretary and a Louis XV open armchair.

EVERY SURFACE IN THIS HALL-WAY HAS BEEN REINTERPRETED BY ARTIST ANDY HOLLAND, LEFT. THE LEAF-ENTWINED LATTICEWORK AND WALLPAPER BORDER WERE ACTUALLY HAND-PAINTED, AS WERE THE BIRD'S-EYE MAPLE DOORS AND MARQUETRY FLOOR.

A PIANO INLAID WITH SUCH STONES AS TIGER'S EYE, LAPIS LAZULI, AND ALPINE VERDE MARBLE IS NOT A VIABLE POSSI-BILITY IN THE REAL WORLD, BUT THOMAS MASARYK CRE-ATED A CONVINCING FANTASY VERSION, OPPOSITE. HE PRO-DUCED THE EFFECT WITH PAINT WITHOUT SACRIFICING THE MUSICAL PERFORMANCE OF THE INSTRUMENT.

A Manhattan wine con-
noisseur is visually transported to French wine
country by gazing at this
mural created by Ever-
greene Studios, carefully
rendered within the laws
of perspective. The be-
lievability of the design is
enhanced by the "balcony"
in the foreground.

WHEN LOOKED AT HEAD ON, THIS STEEL CHAIR SEEMS INCOMPLETE. ONLY WHEN OBSERVED FROM AN ANGLE DO VIEWERS REALIZE THAT A PORTION OF ITS BACK EXISTS ONLY AS A PAINTED IMAGE. CHRISTIAN THEE MADE THE EFFECT ALL THE MORE CREDIBLE WITH THE ADDITION OF A SHOREBIRD PERCHED ON THE CHAIR BACK.

Contemporary needs can also be accommodated as authentic pieces are reproduced and adapted to fit modern purposes. The McMillen Collection includes a black lacquer bed that is based on one that was originally twin-sized; it has been expanded to queen to fit today's taste. Media cabinets, designed to hide televisions and audio equipment unknown before the twentieth century, come in styles to blend seamlessly with any decor. Habersham Plantation produces one inspired by Shaker furniture, Henredon offers one with an antique oriental motif, and Hickory KayLyn's American Artech group has an elegant mid-eighteenth-century Queen Anne–inspired highboy of bird's-eye maple with marquetry detailing.

OFTEN IT IS EASIER FOR DECO-
RATIVE PAINTERS TO REPRO-
DUCE AN EFFECT THAN IT IS TO
REPLACE OR ADD TO EXISTING
MATERIAL. PAXWELL PAINTING
STUDIOS, INC. PAINTED THE
WOODWORK IN THIS ROOM TO
MATCH MAHOGANY, ABOVE.

A FAUX MARBRE TABLE FITS PER-
FECTLY INTO THIS ALCOVE
FILLED WITH CUSHIONS, RIGHT.
JANE E. MILLETT TRANS-
FORMED A MAKESHIFT COFFEE
TABLE INTO THIS IMPRESSIVE
AND EXPENSIVE-LOOKING
PIECE OF FURNITURE.

Bringing authentically realized period furniture into our interiors offers us a chance to live out our fantasies, to provide a setting that supports our image of ourselves, and to do it all economically and practically. For those who wish to re-create the look of an old English library in the family room, Naugahyde may be a more practical choice than leather, especially if there are children or pets in the home. In our living rooms, reproduction rather than authentic Louis XVI furniture provides historic grandeur without the actual ravages of age. As we savor our afternoon tea, settled deep in a chintz-covered armchair, we may survey the scene of our estate laid out for us through the magic of trompe l'oeil, forgetting the dingy street scene that really lies beyond our walls. Such are the joys of creating multidimensional illusions in the home.

ILLUSIONISM AS FASHION AND ACCESSORIES

As Shakespeare says, "All the world's a stage, and all the men and women merely players." The strategies of imitation, re-production, and re-creation help to create the setting for us to act out the roles we have chosen to play; our clothes become our costumes. Geoffrey Squire in *Dress Art and Society* writes that, "dress, quite as much as buildings, books, or pictures, can be a manifestation of man's urgent desire to express ideas and satisfy his mental needs."

CLOTHING AS AN EXPRESSION OF ROLE-PLAYING BEGINS WITH THE FANCIFUL CLOTHING OF CHILDHOOD AS DESIGNED BY KATE HERMAN FOR ETAK.

Fabrics are a fabulous means of transforming everyday accessories and objects into fantasy items. Clockwise from top, a collection of objects are not what they seem: Mé Lo's totes and purses have a safari theme; zebra and tiger prints from Clarence House are a delightful alternative to the real thing; and fake leathers from International Fabrics can be used as clothing or furniture coverings.

IMITATION OF LIFE

With illusionism we have created a setting that fits our fantasies and dressed to play the right part. It's only natural that we would want to populate our environment with images of ourselves. By cloning ourselves, we can exert control over a situation. We can create a cutout of a guard to "patrol" the castle or use a wax figure to entertain us or a mannequin to display the latest fashion.

TWENTIETH-CENTURY ARTISTS HAVE DISPLAYED A PENCHANT FOR CREATING IMAGES AND SCULPTURE THAT MIMIC PEOPLE. THE IMPACT OF J. SEWARD JOHNSON'S LIFE-SIZE AND EXTREMELY REALISTIC BRONZE SCULPTURES IS HEIGHTENED BY THEIR PLACEMENT IN PLAUSIBLE SITUATIONS, NEAR LEFT, TOP AND BOTTOM. CREATED BY THE ARTIST ALEX KATZ IN 1968, A CUTOUT OF A HUMAN FIGURE IS PAINTED ALUMINUM, FAR LEFT. THOUGH ITS QUALITY IS THREE DIMENSIONAL, THE FIGURE COULDN'T BE MISTAKEN FOR A REAL PERSON. BY CONTRAST, THE HIGHLY NATURAL COLOR OF JOHN DeANDREA'S STANDING FEMALE NUDE MAKES IT A DISORIENTING EXPERIENCE FOR AN UNSUSPECTING VIEWER, RIGHT.

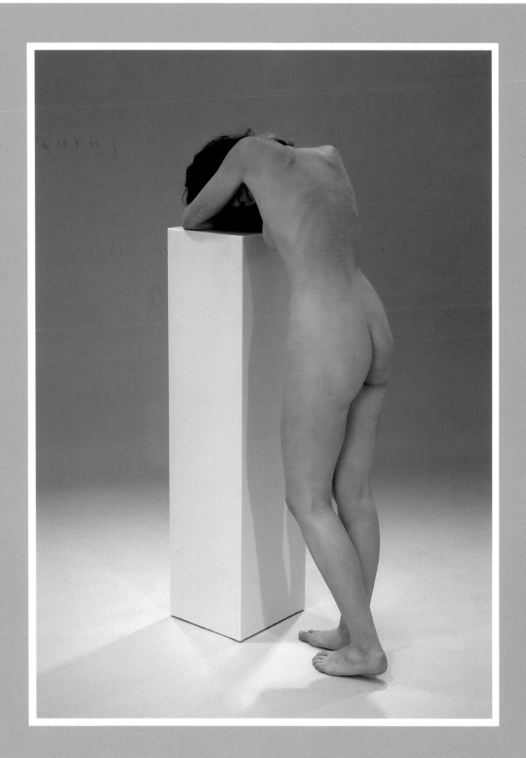

EXTERIORS:
IT'S ALL A FACADE

A drive along the residential streets of any town should be enough to convince us of the pervasiveness of illusionistic architecture. We find a Tudor house next to a Georgian one or maybe the columns are meant to imitate the Southern Plantation style. A Cape Cod saltbox shows up in Phoenix and the stuccoed facade of a Spanish hacienda in Seattle. Or a Victorian home can be restored with low-maintenance aluminum siding and gingerbread from Vintage Wood Works or Renovators Supply or any of the myriad companies catering to the needs of preservationists and re-creationists.

Just as interiors communicate personality so do exteriors. And because creating an impressive facade is invariably more expensive than creating a room, exteriors rely even more on illusionism and enhance the home in a different way: by

THOUGH IT LOOKS LIKE AN ITALIAN VILLA, THIS BUILDING IS ACTUALLY LOCATED IN SAN ANTONIO, TEXAS. THE ROUNDED ARCADE, CORINTHIAN COLUMNS, AND OCULUS WINDOWS ARE ALL CLASSICAL DETAILS THAT BELIE THE BUILDING'S ORIGINS.

setting the scene and providing a visual preview of—and sometimes contrast to—the home's interior. Whether the effect is one of economical grandeur or of grand economy, it can all be done illusionistically.

Again, we look back to ancient Egypt to find a starting place. In the First Dynasty in Egypt (c. 3100–2890 B.C.), glazed or plastered bricks decorated to imitate reed matting were attached as a veneer to walls. In Dynasty III (c. 2682–2613 B.C.), the earlier brick-and-wood buildings were translated into stone, the mason imitating columns of mud-plastered bundles of reeds, palm-log ceilings, and mud-brick walls as well as wooden picket fences and doors. Although the architectural forms themselves harked back to earlier and more humble materials, the use of stone here insured permanence and imparted grandeur.

SERLIO'S THEORY THAT ROUGHLY HEWN STONE CAN REPRESENT THE POWER OF NATURE AND SYMBOLIZE CIVIL POWERS TAKES FORM IN THE RENAISSANCE PALAZZO PITTI IN FLORENCE, ABOVE.

HALLMARKS OF ROMAN CLASSICISM—SYMMETRY, DORIC CAPITALS, AND PLAIN PEDIMENTS—DIGNIFY THIS FEDERAL-STYLE HOUSE IN BATH, MAINE, RIGHT. THE IMAGERY OF THE FEDERAL STYLE WAS ADOPTED IN AMERICA TO LINK THE COUNTRY'S PROSPERITY WITH THE PAST GLORY OF ANCIENT GREECE AND ROME.

The Egyptians may have been the first to suffer from the *edifice complex*. Roughly, this term defines our feeling of awe, even of intimidation, when we confront an imposing building. This is what Augustus was aiming for in Rome. It is said he boasted that he had found a city of brick and left one of marble. Of course, this was an illusion as the brick was really still there under thin marble slabs. The less august Roman citizen also sought to upgrade the appearance of his dwelling. Less pretentious Roman houses were veneered with stucco smoothed over rubble to suggest stonework.

In the Renaissance this same rough-hewn appearance was promoted by the architectural theorist Serlio as a symbol of the force and strength of nature. Using the plaster techniques of ancient Rome, the rustic look was economically created; the wealthier, Florentine architects "rusticated" the

WHEN THE THUNDERBIRD FIRE & SAFETY EQUIPMENT CORPORATION PLANNED A NEW BUILDING IN PHOENIX, ARIZONA, THE OWNER COMMISSIONED RICHARD HAAS TO DECORATE IT. BEFORE HAAS BEGAN, THE STRUCTURE WAS ESSENTIALLY A FEATURELESS STUCCO BOX, ABOVE. THE ARTIST'S WORK TRANSFORMED THE BUILDING INTO A 1880S FANTASY FIREHOUSE, REMINISCENT OF HENRY HOBSON RICHARDSON'S NINETEENTH-CENTURY ARCHITECTURE, RIGHT.

ground-floor facades of urban palazzi with quarried stone blocks roughed up with chisels to give the rounded, pitted look of "natural" rocks.

One of the most inexpensive and effective materials for imitative construction is concrete. A combination of mortar, gravel, and bits of rubble, it was invented in the Near East at least a thousand years before Christ.

In the modern era, concrete has become the basis for much illusionistic construction. Poured in place, it can be colored and imprinted with gridded and radiated patterns. A boon to builders, an unskilled laborer can emboss large areas in a single day. Fiberglass form-liners can also mold concrete to resemble wood. One company has offered twenty-three kinds of wood patterns including "rough-sawn random plank," "wide, rough circular-sawn plank," and aged barn wood. In Japan and elsewhere, park benches have been made from cast concrete imitating logs.

William Randolph Hearst's San Simeon was designed by Julia Morgan, who used concrete to create a fantastic castle. The exterior was cast in reinforced concrete and faced with white stone. Gothic columns defined the main doorway and the facade was decorated with late Gothic Spanish limestone figures and cast-stone ornaments. While no one model or style was used, the overall effect at San Simeon is of absolute grandeur and much of it was achieved illusion-istically.

Morgan's teacher and friend, Bernard Maybeck, was also a talented illusionist. He created grand effects (for example, the automobile showrooms he designed in the 1920s as Roman

AT WILLIAM RANDOLPH HEARST'S SAN SIMEON, WHICH WAS DESIGNED BY JULIA MORGAN, THE NEPTUNE POOL REFLECTS A PASTICHE OF GRECO-ROMAN ARCHITECTURAL ELEMENTS.

temples and Romanesque churches) and often used imitative and innovative construction materials to do it. His friend John A. Rice had invented a lightweight, air-entrained concrete called "Bubblestone" that was fire resistant and inexpensive. Maybeck experimented with it in a one-room house built as a studio for himself in 1924.

To cover a conventional wood-stud frame house, he strung on horizontal wires

ALTHOUGH ARCHITECT MOR-
GAN MODELED SAN SIMEON
AFTER AN ACTUAL SPANISH
CHURCH, THE BUILDING IS NOT
A SLAVISH COPY, BUT A FANTASY
INTERPRETATION.

III

195

burlap bags saturated in the Bubblestone mixture. The hardened concrete created an exterior still serviceable more than fifty years later. Window openings, corners, and flarings were easy to create by cutting or modelling the material while still wet. It required no skilled labor and produced an interesting rustic texture. Colored a deep plum and resembling an English cottage's thatched roof, Bubblestone was also used by Maybeck for a roof on a 1927 house.

Rice was unable to secure the patent rights for Bubblestone and it never caught on. However, the commercial veneers marketed as "Permastone" and "Cultured Stone" did. After World War II, veneer salesmen enticed homeowners to revamp their properties with contractor-applied facings of colored and molded concrete. As in ancient Rome, the fake stone facades present a face of prosperity and strength that says the homeowners are solid citizens.

While one of illusionism's virtues is its ability to preserve an effect forever, another one is that it can also be temporary. Sometimes the illusion of stability and splendor need not be permanent. Illusionism offers a low-cost way to create the appearance of magnificence for a moment.

For the international expositions, popular in the nineteenth century, the grandeur of marble was often created in less expensive materials. Using plaster, the architectural firm of McKim Mead and White built a metropolis of classical temples for the Chicago World's Columbian Exposition of 1893.

As we have already seen, illusionism goes hand in hand with revivalism. Architects have looked to the past for models for the appearance of buildings. Certainly the Founding Fathers of the United

A BACKDROP PAINTED BY GILLIAN BRADSHAW-SMITH OF ATMOSPHERICS IMITATES CONCRETE IN A TROMPE-L'OEIL TWIST. HERE, THE EXTRAORDINARY STANDS IN FOR THE ORDINARY.

States thought this wise, as a trip to the nation's capital confirms. The classical orders allowed them to identify the new country with the great democracy of Greece and the Roman republic.

The suitability of a building's appearance to its purpose is certainly one of the major impetuses for illusionism. In the nineteenth century opera houses and theaters were built in a Beaux-Arts interpretation of the Renaissance and Baroque periods, considered cultural high points. Museums have frequently taken on the appearance of classical temples with art as the object of worship; the buildings themselves were to be edifying, contributing to the aesthetic experience.

A similar rationale has been employed for similar purposes for another art form in the twentieth century. The grand movie theaters of the 1920s and 1930s were lavish edifices designed to enhance the pa-

trons' experience of the illusions they were watching on the silver screen. Theaters were built with one purpose only— to attract moviegoers—and their exteriors, as well as their lush interiors, did that. Theater chain owner Marcus Loew's motto was "We sell tickets to theaters, not movies."

While movie theaters of that golden era were designed to get people out of the house and out of their reality, the desire for a fantasy life also operates domestically. Whether we are a William Randolph Hearst wanting a medieval/Renaissance pile or someone with a more modest budget and a vision of Colonial America, illusionism can help.

Contemporary home buyers can choose from the entire history of architecture for their own dream domiciles. Architects have obliged their clients' whims and their own aesthetic biases for centuries by borrowing, copying, interpreting, and

Marbleized and gilt neoclassical columns distinguish this entryway by Jill Pilaroscia, above. The painted treatments create the illusion of precious materials while eliminating the expense.

For a restaurant with a Roman theme, Born of Brush created a faux bronze door. The rivets and panels are all illusionistically rendered, right.

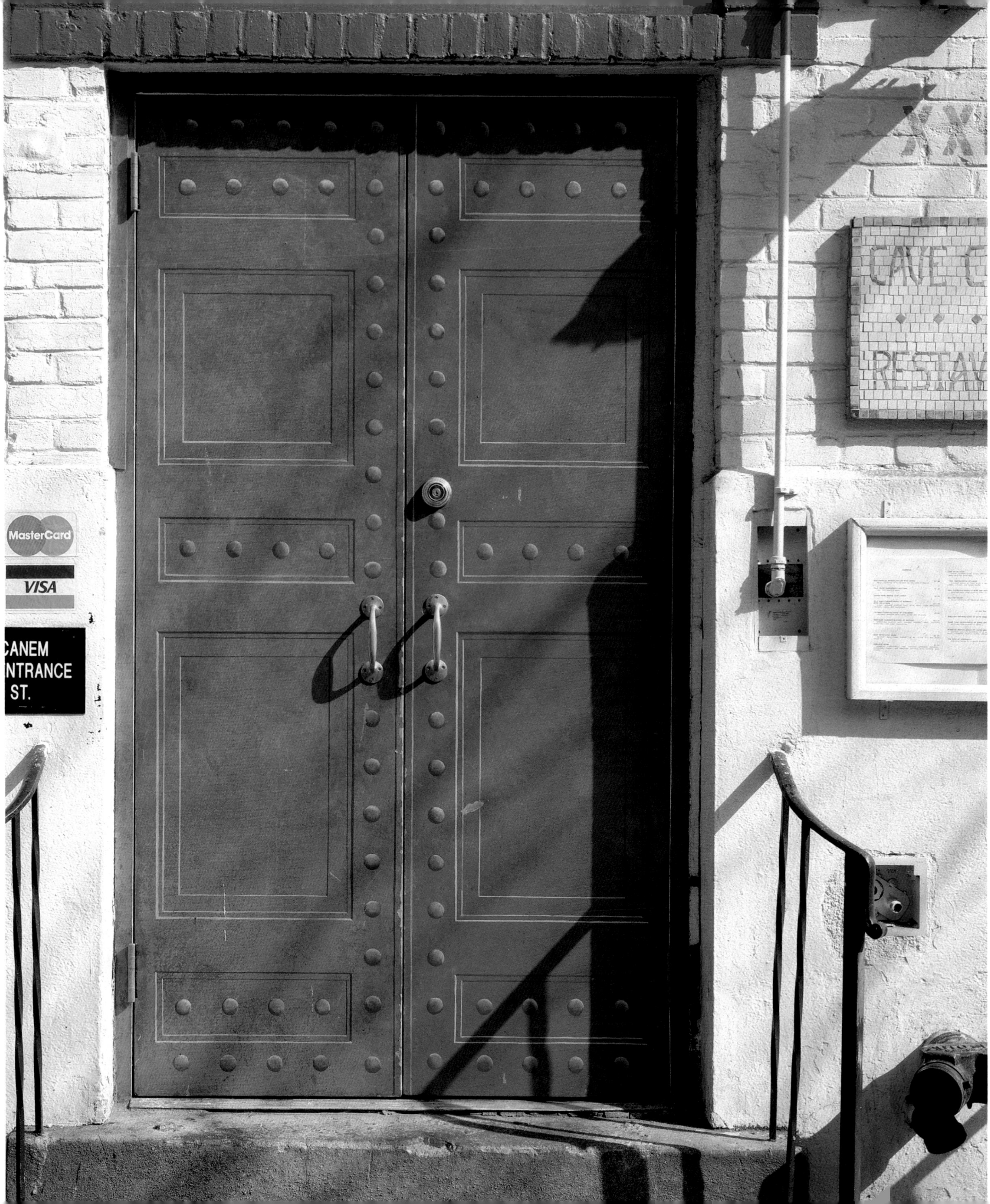
MasterCard
VISA
CANEM
NTRANCE
ST.

A PREVIOUSLY PLAIN MANHATTAN BUILDING WAS IMBUED WITH NEOCLASSICAL OVERTONES BY BORN OF BRUSH. THE DOORWAY IS FLANKED BY COLUMNS AND CROWNED WITH AN ARCHWAY; THE WALLS ARE ENLIVENED BY AN ARCHITECTURAL NICHE SUPPORTING A WATERBEARER.

reinterpreting historical styles.

As an example, the Ecole des Beaux-Arts–trained Morgan built in a variety of architectural styles she considered suitable for their settings: California Spanish Mission for arid areas, Bavarian for the mountains around Tahoe and Shasta, and the contemporary Arts and Crafts style for the rolling hills of the Bay Area. Her mentor, Maybeck, could build a Teutonic Gothic castle for Phoebe Hearst or a Swiss chalet for a Berkeley client without feeling aesthetically compromised.

More recently David Anthony Easton has designed a Georgian-era house for a family in Illinois. Built with modern materials, sometimes "aged" artificially, it faithfully reproduces in appearance, plan, and room arrangement an authentic eighteenth-century home while still accommodating the conveniences and necessities of the twentieth—air conditioning, central heating, electricity. The details are historically correct and the furniture is either authentic or reproduction. Witold Rybczynski writes that "it is neither a copy of a specific house nor a modern 'version' of a historical style. Nor is it an interpretation of the past. Rather, it is the work of an architect from the eighteenth century who, somehow, has found himself in the American Midwest in the twentieth."

Today, even without the help of a talented architect, we can get historical accuracy. Mike Tecton's Custom Homes offers house plans for Georgian, Cape Cod, and Southern Colonial as well as a special collection of Tudor details. If you prefer a romantic cottage instead, you can get blueprints for that as well from the Cottage Collection.

Not always are exterior illusions three dimensional. Sometimes it is done with trompe-l'oeil painting. Contemporary trompe-l'oeil artists

such as Richard Haas and others have been able to respond to the need to establish bland, boxy structures in many cases. On the blank wall of the seven-story building that now blocks the view of the Fontainebleau Hotel in Miami, Haas painted a vision of the 1952 Morris Lapidus building framed in a triumphal arch.

Martin Filler has called this an example of "urban stagecraft of which any Beaux-Arts–trained architect would be proud, and of which any budget-strapped city planner of our own day should be envious." Haas has become well known for his "architecture of illusion," creating fantasy facades on blank walls.

FOR MARIE ANTOINETTE AND HER COURT, THE ARCHITECT MIQUE BUILT A FULL-SCALE PEASANT VILLAGE AT VERSAILLES, ABOVE. IT WAS A SMALL WORKING FARM, BUT ITS REAL PURPOSE WAS TO ENTERTAIN. THE EXTERIORS WERE RUSTIC, AND IN A SENSE, ILLUSIONARY, AS THE INTERIORS WERE SUMPTUOUSLY DESIGNED.

Whether the illusionism is merely a practicality-based decision to use aluminum siding, the re-creation of a historical style in contemporary materials, or the trompe-l'oeil rendering of what might have been or even was, it continues to serve its masters. The results range from the convincing to the fanciful, but they are always comforting.

THE TURRETS AND TOWERS OF THESE MACKINAC ISLAND HOUSES ARE VICTORIAN MISINTERPRETATIONS OF RENAISSANCE ARCHITECTURE, AND ARE ACTUALLY MORE MEDIEVAL THAN CLASSICAL IN DESIGN, ABOVE.

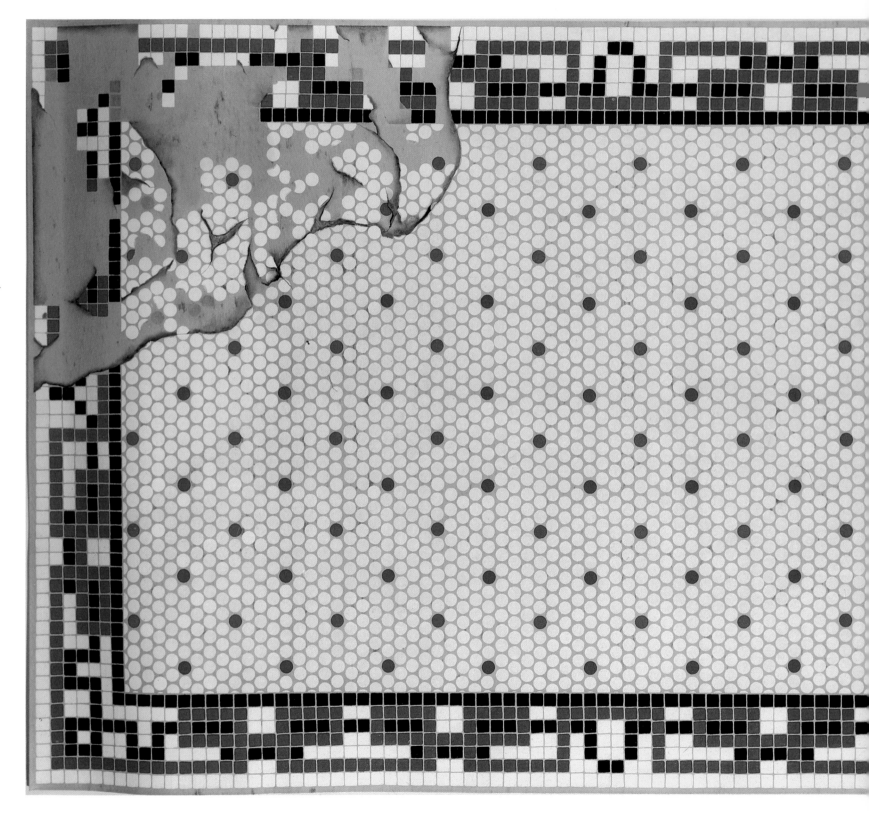

204

AFTERWORD

It is impossible to get through an ordinary day without being exposed to imitations, reproductions, and re-creations. When I leave my apartment, I enter a wood-grained Formica-panelled elevator to emerge into a world filled with objects and panoramas that appear to be something other than they are—such as store windows filled with eighteenth-century reproduction furniture or buildings painted with false windows and architectural details. Rather than being confused by such deliberately misleading scenes, I enjoy the illusions and even welcome them at home. I take pleasure in being able to enlarge my small apartment with a trompe-l'oeil vision of another, grander room. It pleases me that although my bentwood rocker is not really Thonet, it is still a graceful addition to my living room. The vinyl floor in the kitchen is easy to care for and I appreciate that it resembles ceramic tile. Such faux elements actually enhance reality in many cases.

From the time of the Egyptians, altering our homes and properties has enabled us to create the environment we truly desire. Our fantasies have been realized through the innocently deceptive practices of the illusionist, whether a skillful trompe-l'oeil painter or a scientist with a miraculous synthetic product. We have relied on illusionism to give us the effect we desire at a price we can afford. We have opted for convincing imitations and durable reproductions when they outperform the real thing. At the same time, we have turned to fanciful objects and painted effects that play off reality and even re-create it simply to amuse.

In the late twentieth century, instances of illusionism are increasing. Decoration and ornamentation have triumphed over modernist design and the "truth to materials" crowd, returning illusionism to its honored place as a decorative strategy. Technology is creating new and better substitutes. We are able to create synthetic materials in imitation of essentially all of those occurring naturally. We are also more aware of the past—both the grand and the modest—and are actively trying to preserve it. When the authentic is inaccessible (too far away or too expensive), we can re-create it.

Illusionism has been around for millennia, and I think I can safely say that it will always remain a vital part of our lives. We will continue to rely on illusions until the real world lives up to our fantasies. And, in the meantime, we may be all the better for it.

—K.S.C.,
New York City, 1991

206

208

SOURCES

ARTISTS FOR HIRE
APPLIED ARTISTS

Illusionistic decorative techniques have been used for thousands of years. Until the twentieth century it was common for architects to use illusionistic strategies, calling on skilled decorative artists to alleviate problems such as excess weight or expense with faux marbre or to create a fantasy environment to delight their patrons. In this century with the Modernist school of architecture denouncing the use of ornament and extolling the virtues of unadulterated materials such as steel and concrete, illusionism seemed not only an antiquated idea but also a morally repugnant one. The latest classical revival—Post-Modernism—has changed that. Decoration is in again and illusionism is being restored to a legitimate place in the artist's and designer's repertoire. In the last ten years, an increasing number of decorators and architects have turned to illusion to create the effects that would be otherwise impossible.

Because of this interest in decorative painting techniques, the market now supports thousands of artisans of varying degrees of education and skill. Training can range from self-taught to degrees from prestigious European academies. While individual craftspersons may be adept at a variety of techniques, they frequently specialize in particular effects. For example, a painter who excels in creating delightfully whimsical vistas may not be so facile in imitating wood graining.

There is no professional organization for these decorative artists. Many advertise in magazines reporting on design and architecture. Many others rely on word of mouth to promote their business. Local interior designers and architects can also offer suggestions. If you are interested in hiring a professional, the following list can give you a starting place.

LESLEY ACHITOFF
160 West End Ave.
New York, NY 10023
212 724-8020

ARTE FACTUM
INCORPORATED
2 Wooster St.
New York, NY 10013
212 431-6743

ATMOSPHERICS
113 Willow Ave.
Hoboken, NJ 07030
201 659-8537

CHRISTINE BELFOR
DESIGN LTD.
177 E. 87th St., Studio 402
New York, NY 10128
212 722-5410
ceramic tile

ZULEYKA BENITEZ
4750 N. Dover
Chicago, IL 60640
312 275-3289

ANDREA M. BIGGS
TIMOTHY G. BIGGS
792 Eastern Pkwy.
Brooklyn, NY 11213
718 771-4221

BORN OF BRUSH
163 Ludlow Street
New York, NY 10002
212 529-3364

CHELSEA SURFACES
70A Greenwich Ave., Ste. 108
New York, NY 10011
212 691-6611

DAVID COHN
240 Waverly Pl.
New York, NY 10014
212 741-3548

VIRGINIA CRAWFORD
285 W. Broadway, Studio 310
New York, NY 10013
212 226-6259

DECORATIVE ARTS, LTD.
2011 S. Shepherd
Houston, TX 77019
713 520-1680

MIRIAM ELLNER SURFACE
DESIGN
161 W. 75th St.
New York, NY 10023
212 874-4493

EON ARTS
457 Broome St.
New York, NY 10013
212 941-1170

EVERGREENE PAINTING
STUDIOS, INC.
635 W. 23rd St.
New York, NY 10011
212 727-9500

FINISHING TOUCHES
2532 Broadway
New York, NY 10025
212 932-3931

DAVID FISCH STUDIOS
1014 S. Main St.
Spring Valley, NY 10977
212 989-8773

BECKY FRANCO
58 Richards Rd.
Port Washington, NY 11050
516 883-2198

MARK GIGLIO
233 Elizabeth St., No. 21
New York, NY 10012
212 431-8926

RICHARD GILLETTE
STEPHEN SHADLEY
144 W. 27th St.
New York, NY 10001
212 226-3850
or
407 Greenwich St.
New York, NY 10013
212 243-6913

GRAND ILLUSION
DECORATIVE
PAINTING INC.
368 Broadway, #503
New York, NY 10013
212 285-0542

GRANDES ILLUSIONS
STUDIOS
264 Bowery
New York, NY 10012
212 966-5301

CHARLES GOFORTH
666 West End Avenue, #7S
New York, NY 10025
212 362-8355

LYNN GOODPASTURE
42 W. 17th St.
New York, NY 10011
212 645-5334

ANNE GRAY HARRIS
DESIGN STUDIO
114 W. 29th St.
New York, NY 10001
212 594-0293

CHUCK HETTINGER
105 Ave. B
New York, NY 10009
212 777-7700

ANDY HOLLAND
208 E. 7th St., #26
New York, NY 10009
212 505-9176

TOM ISBELL
ISBELL & ELLIOTT
ARTISANS
156 E. 102nd St.
New York, NY 10029
212 536-6476

TED SETH JACOBS
523 E. 83rd St.
New York, NY 10028
212 737-9212

ROBERT JACKSON
Box 117
Germantown, NY 12526
518 828-1805

ANNIE KELLY
6938 Camrose Dr.
Los Angeles, CA 90068
213 876-5374

LILLIAN KENNEDY
319 Park Pl.
Brooklyn, NY 11238
718 622-2840

NANCY A. KINTISCH
89 Bridge St.
Brooklyn, NY 11201
718 935-9019
718 797-5729

KAREN LUKAS
18 N. Moore St,
New York, NY 10013
212 431-8164

CARLOS MARCHIORI
357 Frederick St.
San Francisco, CA 94117
415 564-6671

MAER-MURPHY INC.
429 W. 53rd St.
New York, NY 10019
212 265-3460

PAMELA MARGONELLI
66 Thomas St.
New York, NY 10013
212 233-0559

THOMAS MASARYK
3016 Philip Ave.
Bronx, NY 10465
212 823-5440

JANE MILLETT
10 Downing St.
New York, NY 10014
212 924-6263

LUCRETIA MORONI
320 E. 57th St.
New York, NY 10022
212 888-0071

RICHARD LOWELL NEAS
157 E. 71st St.
New York, NY 10021
212 772-1878

PAXWELL PAINTING
STUDIOS, INC.
223 E. 32nd St.
New York, NY 10016
212 725-1737

EDWARD K. PERRY
COMPANY
53 Plain St.
Braintree, MA 02184
617 849-9810

DOUGLAS RISEBOROUG
217 Ashland Ave.
Santa Monica, CA 90405
213 399-4990

ANTONIO ROMANO
480 Broadway
New York, NY 10012
212 941-1452

EDWARD SCHMIDT
The New York Academy
    of Art
419 Lafayette St.
New York, NY 10003
212 505-5300

JAMES ALAN SMITH
153 E. 88th St., #8
New York, NY 10128
212 876-4660

STRACKBEIN & BRABY
306 President St.
Brooklyn, NY 11231
718 625-3735

THE STUDIO
12 Engle St., Ste. 201
Englewood, NJ 07631
201 569-9114

CHRISTIAN THEE
49 Old Stagecoach Rd.
Weston, CT 06883
203 454-0340

MICHAEL THORNTON–
SMITH
123 Chambers St.
New York, NY 10007
212 619-5338

TROMPLOY, INC.
400 Lafayette St.
New York, NY 10003
212 420-1639

VIRGINIA DESIGNS
285 W. Broadway, Ste. 310
New York, NY 10012
212 226-6259

ROBERT WALKER
1825 Stanford St.
Santa Monica, CA 90404
213 453-1384

SCOTT WATERMAN
266 B Oxford Pl. N.E.
Atlanta, GA 30307
404 373-9438

OTHER CRAFTSPEOPLE

EPPING'S TAXIDERMY AND
ART STUDIO
R.R. 9, Box 522
Winchester, VA 22601
703 665-0703

DAVID FLAHARTY,
SCULPTOR
402 Magazine Rd., R.D. #2
Green Lane, PA 18054
215 234-8242
ornamental plaster, fiberglass,
bronze, and concrete center-
pieces and cornices

F.B. FOGG
3208 Burlington
Muncie, IN 47302
317 289-7464
cast paper architectural
details

F. WARD GAINES
P.O. Box 21622
Washington, DC 20009
202 265-2682
cast polyester resin "mosaics"

MATTHEW
SZCZEPANOWSKI
1820 Callowhill St.
Philadelphia, PA 19130
215 569-8638
plaster, cement, bronze details

S.R. WHITE
CARVING SHOP
R.D. 3, Box 71A
Jacks Creek Rd.
Lewistown, PA 17044
717 242-1752
duck decoys

FINE ARTISTS

Many fine artists base their work on the play between illusion and reality. For some this involves highly realistic renderings. Others use abstract imagery to create optical illusions, either two-dimensionally or three-dimensionally. Many are represented by galleries, which will periodically present their work in exhibitions, but which also generally keep a number of representative pieces in the gallery storerooms. Galleries also maintain a photographic archive of work that may be available for sale. Many of these artists also accept commissions.

JOHN AHEARN
Brooke Alexander Gallery
50 Wooster St.
New York, NY 10012
212 925-4338
realistic figurative sculpture

DOUG ANDERSON
Heller Gallery
71 Greene St.
New York, NY 10012
212 966-5948
pâte-de-verre glass castings

RICHARD ARTSCHWAGER
Leo Castelli Gallery
420 W. Broadway
New York, NY 10012
212 431-5160
sculpture using Formica and
Celotex, often derived from
furniture shapes

MIKE BIDLO
Leo Castelli Gallery
421 W. Broadway
New York, NY 10012
212 431-5160
paintings in the spirit of other
well-known artists such as
Jackson Pollock and Pablo
Picasso

WENDELL CASTLE
Alexander F. Milliken Gallery
98 Prince St.
New York, NY 10012
212 966-7800
wood furniture with trompe-
l'oeil elements

JOHN DEANDREA
Carlo Lamagna Gallery
50 W. 57th St.
New York, NY 10019
212 245-6006
life-size figurative sculpture
in cast polymer

STEVEN DEVRIES
Heller Gallery
71 Greene St.
New York, NY 10012
212 966-5948
glass sculptures that are
optically deceiving

JUDY FOX
Carlo Lamagna Gallery
50 W. 57th St.
New York, NY 10019
212 245-6006
terra cotta figurative
sculpture

RICHARD HAAS
361 W. 36th St.
New York, NY 10018
212 947-9868
trompe-l'oeil paintings

DUANE HANSON
O.K. Harris Works of Art
383 W. Broadway
New York, NY 10012
212 431-3600
life-size figurative sculpture

J. SEWARD JOHNSON, JR.
Sculpture Placement
P.O. Box 9709
Washington, DC 20016
202 362-9310
life-size figurative sculpture

TONY KING
O.K. Harris Works of Art
383 W. Broadway
New York, NY 10012
212 431-3600
large-scale paintings of
currency

JUSTEN LADDA
112 Stanton St.
New York, NY 10002
212 228-6548
paintings and installations
based on one-point
perspective

MARILYN LEVINE
O.K. Harris Works of Art
383 W. Broadway
New York, NY 10012
212 431-3600
ceramic sculpture of leather
objects

FLORA C. MACE AND JOEY
KIRKPATRICK
2107 N. 34th St.
Seattle, WA 98102
206 632-7080
glass fruits and vegetables

SYLVIA PLIMACK
MANGOLD
Brooke Alexander Gallery
50 Wooster St.
New York, NY 10012
212 925-4338
paintings with trompe-l'oeil
elements

MEGAN PARRY
1300 E. Lafayette, #907
Detroit, MI 48207
313 567-3323
paintings with distorted
perspectives

CURT ROYSTON
18 Desbrosses St.
New York, NY 10013
212 431-3563
painted installations that
make three-dimensional
objects appear two-
dimensional

PAUL STANKARD
Heller Gallery
71 Greene St.
New York, NY 10012
212 966-5948
paperweights of highly
realistic wildflowers

JOHN TORREANO
Shea & Beker Gallery
20 W. 57th St.
New York, NY 10019
212 974-8100
paintings using glass jewels

FUMIO YOSHIMURA
139 Academy Rd.
Phetford Center, VT 05075
802 649-5118
wood carvings of mundane
objects

CREATE YOUR OWN ILLUSIONS
SCHOOLS

With the burgeoning interest in faux finishes, many people have
become interested in learning the craft, either for their own use or
professionally. A number of schools and community centers offer
classes in illusionistic techniques.

DAY STUDIO VIDEOS
1504P Bryant St.
San Francisco, CA 94103
415 626-9300

FASHION INSTITUTE OF
TECHNOLOGY
Seventh Ave. at 27th St.
New York, NY 10001
212 760-7700

FE FI FAUX, INC.
337 S. Davie St.
Greensboro, NC 27401
919 272-3289

THE FINISHING SCHOOL
17 Maple Dr.
Great Neck, NY 11021
516 487-2270

THE NEW SCHOOL FOR
SOCIAL RESEARCH
66 W. 12th St.
New York, NY 10011
212 741-5690
classes in surface decoration
including faux finishes and
trompe l'oeil

ISABEL O'NEIL
FOUNDATION FOR THE
ART OF THE PAINTED
FINISH
177 E. 87th St.
New York, NY 10128
212 348-2120

THE STUDIO, FINE AND
DECORATIVE ARTS
12 Engle St., Ste. 201
Englewood, NJ 07631
201 569-9114

TROMPLOY INC.
400 Lafayette St.
New York, NY 10003
212 420-1639

FAUX FINISHES IN A KIT

Stores specializing in housewares and hardware offer a full range of products to help you do it yourself; the following are just a few of those available.

COUNTRY COLORS FAUX
FINISH DECORATING
GLAZE
Illinois Bronze Paint Co.
300 E. Main St.
Lake Zurich, IL 60047
708 438-8201
for wood, tinware, preprimed
canvas

FLECK STONE
Plasti-Kote Co.
P.O. Box 708
Medina, OH 44258-0708
216 725-4511
faux granite spray

FRENCH WASH FAUX
FINISH
MARBLEIZING KIT
Plaid Enterprises Inc.
1649 International Blvd.
Norcross, GA 30091
404 923-8200
for flat painted surfaces

PATINA GREEN
Modern Options
888 Brannan St.
San Francisco, CA 94103
415 243-0357
master finishing solution for
the reproduction of antique
verdigris surface on copper,
brass, or bronze

ILLUSIONISM FOR SALE
REPRODUCTION FURNITURE

Retail furniture showrooms across the country feature chairs, beds, chests, etc., reproducing historical styles. They vary in degrees of authenticity and are available in every price range. Some furniture manufacturers such as Shaker Workshops concentrate on a particular style while others, such as Lane and Baker, produce a wide variety. Smaller workshops may focus on one particular item; for example, Frederick Dackloe and Bros. specializes in Windsor chairs.

The following listing includes retail showrooms and corporate headquarters for a number of large manufacturers of reproduction furniture as well as smaller studios and individual craftsmakers. The company's main office can give you the name of a retail outlet in your vicinity.

ETHAN ALLEN
2490 Summer St.
Stamford, CT 06905
203 356-9613

A. ANDERSON
164 William St.
New York, NY 10038
212 571-0258
Stickley reproductions

E.J. AUDI
317 E. 34th St.
New York, NY 10016
212 679-7580
Stickley reproductions

BAKER FURNITURE
COMPANY
1661 Monroe Ave. N.W.
Grand Rapids, MI 49505
616 361-7321

THE BARTLEY
COLLECTION LIMITED
3 Airpark Dr.
Easton, MD 21601
301 820-7722
Queen Anne furniture kits

BERNDHARDT
Box 740
Lenoir, NC 28645
800 345-9875

FREDERICK DACKLOE &
BROS.
P.O. Box 427
Portland, PA 18351
Windsor chairs

DREXEL HERITAGE
1690 English Rd.
High Point, NC 28619
919 889-2501
800 447-4700

GRANGE U.S.A.
200 Lexington Ave.
New York, NY 10016
212 685-9057

GRANGE BOUTIQUE
831 Madison Ave.
New York, NY 10021
212 737-8080

PETER FRANKLIN
1 Cottage St.
P.O. Box 1166 A
Easthampton, MA 01027
413 527-4004
Windsor chairs

HABERSHAM PLANTATION
CORP.
P.O. Box 1209
Toccoa, GA 30577
404 886-1476

HENREDON FURNITURE
INDUSTRIES, INC.
P.O. Box 70
Morganton, NC 28655
705 437-5261

HICKORY KAYLYN
P.O. Box 998
Hickory, NC 28603
704 322-8624

R. HOOD & CO.
R.F.D. 3, College Rd.
Meredith, NH 03253
603 279-8607
early American furniture

IRVING & JONES
Village Center
Colebrook, CT 06021
203 379-9219

THE LANE CO. INC.
Altavista, VA 24517-0151
800 447-2882

LEONARD'S
600 Taunton Ave.
Seekonk, MA 02771
508 336-8585

RALPH LAUREN
550 Seventh Ave.
New York, NY 10018
212 221-0675

MARTHA M. HOUSE
1022 S. Decatur St.
Montgomery, AL 36104
205 264-3558
Victorian furniture

PHOENIX DESIGN, LTD.
733 N. Wells St.
Chicago, IL 60610
312 951-7945
Modernist furniture by
Le Corbusier, Mies van
der Rohe, MacKintosh

POMPEII
255 N.W. 25th St.
Miami, FL 33127
305 576-3600
aluminum furniture

QUEEN ANNE FURNITURE
CO. INC.
Rt. 2, Box 427
Trinity, NC 27370
919 431-2562
919 434-4990

RMK ASSOCIATES
International Design Center
   New York
Center Two, 5th floor
30-20 Thomson Ave.
Long Island City, NY 11101
718 482-8100
English reproduction
furniture

SHAKER WORKSHOPS
Box 1028
Concord, MA 01743
617 646-8985

STICKLEY FURNITURE
P.O. Box 480
Manlius, NY 13104
315 682-5441

TROPITONE
P.O. Box 3197
Sarasota, FL 34230
800 876-7288
sand-cast aluminum
furniture

VULPIANI WORKSHOP INC.
11 Field Ct.
Kingston, NY 12401
914 339-6146
Stickley furniture

WORKBENCH
470 Park Ave. S.
New York, NY 10016
212 532-7900
Shaker-inspired furniture

REPRODUCTIONS OF FINE ART AND DECORATIVE OBJECTS

Illusionism as a decorative strategy has been utilized since earliest times. Every man-made object, from the most practical to the most frivolous, has the potential to be decorated illusionistically. Department stores, speciality shops, and craft fairs are all filled with merchandise designed to represent something that it's not. Museums are a wonderful source for affordable and tasteful replicas of objects from their own and other collections. Their gift shops frequently stock a large selection of reproductions of paintings, prints, and drawings and of facsimiles of decorative objects and jewelry.

A full listing of all the companies and designers who use illusionistic tactics is simply impossible. However, let us list a few in order to show the range of illusionistic products available in the marketplace today.

ABC CARPET & HOME
888 Broadway
New York, NY 10003
212 473-3000
carpet, tile, furniture
reproductions,
decorative objects

ALVA MUSEUM REPLICAS &
SCULPTURE, INC.
24-49 44th St.
Long Island City, NY 11103
718 278-4006
718 726-4064
reproductions of sculpture
from museum collections

A.P.F., INC.
1625 Bathgate Ave.
Bronx, NY 10457
212 901-1400
800 221-9519
frames

ATTA, INC.
521 W. 26th St.
New York, NY 10001
212 643-2024
realistic human figures

ARTISTIX
Spare Me the Details
    (importer)
29 S. Main St.
Ipswich, MA 01938
508 356-4014
plastic adhesive sheet

CHRISTOFLE ET CIE
680 Madison Ave.
New York, NY 10021
212 308-9390
silver

COLONIAL COLLECTIONS
OF NEW ENGLAND, INC.
202 Idlewood Dr.
Stamford, CT 06905
203 322-0078
decorative objects

COLONIAL WILLIAMSBURG
P.O. Box CH
Williamsburg, VA 23187
800 446-9240
decorative objects

CONTACT PAPER
Rubbermaid
1147 Akron Rd.
Wooster, OH 44691
216 264-6464
plastic adhesive sheet

COOPER-HEWITT MUSEUM
2 E. 91st St.
New York, NY 10028
212 860-6878
Smithsonian Institution's
National Museum of
Design

COUNTRY WOOD
PRODUCTS
510 Second Ave.
Wayland, NY 14572
716 728-5745
decorative objects

H.A. DENUNZIO CO., INC.
Box 470
Springfield, MA 01101-0470
800 222-6827
reproduction paintings

DORFMAN MUSEUM
FIGURES, INC.
1601 Guilford Ave.
Baltimore, MD 21202
301 685-1670
800 634-4873
realistic human figures

DVB-ALVA MUSEUM
JEWELRY
611 Broadway, Ste. 622
New York, NY 10012
212 995-9300
jewelry

EINSTEIN MOOMJY
150 E. 58th St.
New York, NY 10022
212 758-0900
carpet

EuRODESIGN SUPPLY, INC.
P.O. Box 571076
Houston, TX 77257-1076
800 433-6339
marble fruit

FACSIMILES LTD.
1-B Pine St. Extension N.
Nashua, NH 03060
603 889-8880
reproductions of sculptures

FAKSIMILE
152 Mercer St.
New York, NY 10012
212 226-7658
facsimiles of historical
documents

FITZ & FLOYD
225 Fifth Ave.
New York, NY 10010
212 685-1980
china

HUBERT DES FORGES
1193A Lexington Ave.
New York, NY 10028
212 744-1857
towels

FROZEN MOMENTS OF
ASPEN
P.O. Box 419
Aspen, CO 81611
800 252-7736
decorative objects

HANDMADE COLONIAL
LIGHTING
6 Fremont St.
Worcester, MA 01603
508 755-3434
and
Metro W. Plaza
Rte. 20
Marboro, MA 01752
508 485-6721

HISTORICAL DOCUMENTS
CO.
8 N. Preston St.
Philadelphia, PA 19104
215 387-8076
reproductions of
banknotes and other
historical documents

R. HOOD & CO.
R.F.D. 3, College Rd.
Meredith, NH 03253
603 279-8607
early American decorating
supplies and furnishings
including paint, paper,
fabrics, hardware, lighting,
furniture, accessories

JADIS MODERNE
2701 Main St.
Santa Monica, CA 90405
213 396-3477
restored telephones

JANNES ART PUBLISHING
3318 N. Lincoln Ave.
Chicago, IL 60657
312 283-0262
fine art reproductions

LICHTENBERG GRAPHIC
12 W. 96th St.
New York, NY 10025
212 865-4312
fine art reproductions

M&CO.
50 W. 17th St.
New York, NY 10011
212 243-0082
desk accessories

MOTTAHEDEH
225 Fifth Ave.
New York, NY 10010
212 685-3050
reproduction ceramics

MUSEUM OF MODERN ART
DESIGN STORE
44 W. 53rd St.
New York, NY 10019
212 708-9700

NORTH LIGHT SCULPTURE
STUDIO
133 W. Pittsburgh Ave.
Milwaukee, WI 53204
414 273-0898
human figures custom
modeled

ADEL ROOTSTEIN
205 W. 19th St.
New York, NY 10010
212 645-2020
display mannequins

ROSENTHAL CHINAWARE
U.S.A.
41 Madison Ave.
New York, NY 10010
212 696-1846

THE SALTBOX
3004 Columbia Ave.
Lancaster, PA 17603
717 392-5649
lanterns, postlights,
chandeliers

SOICHER-MARIN
11240 Playa Ct.
Culver City, CA 90230
213 390-3418
fine art reproductions

SPITTIN' IMAGE
P.O. Box 1150
Penn Valley, CA 95946
916 432-3545
display figures

STUDIO EIS
90 Fulton St.
New York, NY 10038
718 797-4561
life cast figures

TIFFANY & CO.
Fifth Ave. and 57th St.
New York, NY 10022
800 526-0649
decorative objects

FREDERICK P. VICTORIA
AND SON, INC.
154 E. 55th St.
New York, NY 10022
212 755-2549
antique decorative arts

VICTORIAN LIGHTING
WORKS
251 S. Pennsylvania Ave.
P.O. Box 469
Center Hall, PA 16828
814 364-9577

VINTAGE VALENCES
Box 43326H
Cincinnati, OH 45243
513 561-8665
period draperies

V'SOSKE
155 E. 56th St.
New York, NY 10022-2748
212 688-1150
rugs

BRUNSCHWIG & FILS, INC.
979 Third Ave.
New York, NY 10022-1234
212 838-7878

C & A WALLCOVERINGS
23645 Mercantile Rd.
Cleveland, OH 44122
215 464-3700

CLARENCE HOUSE
211 E. 58th St.
New York, NY 10022
212 752-2890

R. HOOD & CO.
R.F.D. 3, College Rd.
Meredith, NH 03253
603 279-8607

RALPH LAUREN
550 Seventh Ave.
New York, NY 10018
212 221-0675

QUAKER LACE COMPANY
1040 Avenue of the Americas
New York, NY 10018
212 221-0480

ARTHUR SANDERSON &
SONS
979 Third Ave.
New York, NY 10022
212 319-7220

SCALAMANDRÉ
300 Trade Zone Dr.
Ronkonkoma, NY 11779
516 467-8800

F. SCHUMACHER AND CO.
939 Third Ave.
New York, NY 10022
212 415-3900
and
1325 Cooch's Bridge Rd.
Newark, DE 19711
800 523-1200

SUNFLOWER STUDIO
2851 Rd. B 1/2
Grand Junction, CO 81503
303 242-3883

RICHARD E. THIBAULT
INC.
706 S. 21st St.
Irvington, NJ 07111
201 399-7888

WALLCOVERINGS AND FABRICS

Throughout history less expensive substitutes for rich fabrics have
been manufactured, either using cheaper fibers or substituting
paper, as the original wallpapers did, for fabric. Illusionistic devices
such as trompe l'oeil and flocking continue to be used by wallpaper
designers to create a richer effect. Many wallpaper and fabric
manufacturers also reproduce earlier patterns, which can aid the
home owner in re-creating an authentic period look.

BASSETT & VOLLUM
4350 N. Council Hill Rd.
Galena, IL 61036
815 777-2460

BRADBURY & BRADBURY
P.O. Box 155
Benicia, CA 94510
707 746-1900

STANDARD BUILDING PRODUCTS

Architects, interior designers, and building contractors know the
joys of illusionism. From the standpoints of economy and practicality, they have a wide variety of products available to enhance
their clients' environments. Many companies offer vinyl tiling in a
multitude of illusionary effects; GMT Floor Tile, Mannington, Armstrong, Congoleum, Kentile Floors, and Azrock are only a few of
them. Although Formica has become a generic name for plastic
laminates, similar amazing imposters are manufactured by companies such as Du Pont, Wilson Art, and Nevamar. Many of these
products can be found in hardware and paint stores across the
country. In many areas large home centers stock a wide selection of
these and other illusionistic products including wallcoverings and
commercially manufactured architectural details. Magazines such
as *Practical Homeowner* and *Home Handyman* feature articles on
these products and their use.

ARMSTRONG FLOORS
P.O. Box 3001
Lancaster, PA 17604
717 397-0611

CONGOLEUM
989 Lenox Dr.
Lawrenceville, NJ 08648
609 584-3000

DU PONT I.E. DE
NEMOURS & CO.
1007 Market St.
Wilmington, DE 19898
800 441-7515

FORMICA CORP.
Sanford Rd.
Piscataway, NJ
212 964-5778

GMT FLOOR TILE
1255 Oak Point Ave.
Bronx, NY 10474
800 346-8453

KENTILE FLOORS
58 Second Ave.
Brooklyn, NY 11215
718 768-9500

MANNINGTON MILLS INC.
P.O. Box 30
Salem, NJ 08079
609 935-3000

NEVAMAR CORP.
8839 Telegraph Rd.
Odentown, MD 21112
301 569-5000

ROLL-A-TEX
Gamma Laboratories
840 Arroyo Ave.
San Fernando, CA 91340
818 365-7500

TRANS CERAMICA LTD.
P.O. Box 795
Elk Grove, IL 60009
312 350-1555

WILSON ART CO.
5251 Brick Rd.
Carson City, NV 89702
800 433-3222
800 792-6000 (in TX)

ARCHITECTURAL DETAILING

Large factories and individual craftspeople produce moldings, ceilings, fireplace mantles, and every other form of period ornamentation in a variety of materials from wood to cast polymer. Now quaint bathroom fixtures, lighting devices converted from gas to electricity, and "classic" telephones are all available to complete a recreation of an earlier period style room.

AA ABBINGDON
AFFILIATES, INC.
2149 Utica Ave.
Brooklyn, NY 11234
718 258-8333
tin ceilings

ARCHITECTURAL
COMPONENTS
26 N. Leverett Rd.
Montagu, MA 01351
413 367-9441
eighteenth- and
nineteenth-century
millwork

ARISTOCAST ORIGINALS
6200 Highlands Parkway S.E.,
   Ste. 1
Smyrna, GA 30082
404 333-9934
404 333-9935

BALL AND BALL
436 W. Lincoln Hwy.
Exton, PA 19341
215 363-7330
metal reproductions

BATHROOM MACHINERIES
Box 1020-G
Murphys, CA 95247
209 728-2031

CARLISLE RESTORATION
LUMBER
H.C.R. 32
Box 679
Stoddard, NH 03464-9712
603 446-3937
flooring

CHADSWORTH
INCORPORATED
P.O. Box 53268
Atlanta, GA 30355
404 876-5410
wood columns

CHELSEA DECORATIVE
METAL CO.
9603 Moonlight Dr.
Houston, TX 77096
713 721-9200
tin ceilings

COLONIAL WOODWORKS
Box 19965
Raleigh, NC 27619
919 783-5592

DECORATORS SUPPLY
CORPORATION
3610-12 S. Morgan St.
Chicago, IL 60609
312 847-6300
wood, composition, wood
fiber ornaments

FEDERAL CABINET CO.,
INC.
409 Highland Ave.
Box 190
Middletown, NY 10940
914 342-1511
wood turnings

FOCAL POINT, INC.
P.O. Box 93327
Atlanta, GA 30377-0327
800 662-5550
cast polymer architectural
   details

HARTMANN-SANDERS CO.
4340 Bankers Circle
Atlanta, GA 30360
800 241-4303
wood columns

HORTON BRASSES
Nooks Hill Rd.
P.O. Box 120-P
Cromwell, CT 06416
203 635-4400
reproduction hardware

HUGGLER-WYSS
541 Pacific Ave.
Willmar, MN 56201
612 235-6020
custom wood and plaster
ornament

WM. H. JACKSON
COMPANY
3 E. 47th St.
New York, NY 10017
212 PL3-9400
reproduction fireplace
mantles

MASACCO'S INSTANT
TROMPE L'OEIL
109 Thompson St.
New York, NY 10012
212 925-8667
architectural renderings of
columns, capitals,
moldings, etc., on
wallpaper

NATIONAL TRUST FOR
HISTORIC PRESERVATION
MERCHANDISING
DIVISION
1600 H. St. N.W.
Washington, DC 20006
202 673-4201
reproduction of
architectural elements in
National Trust collection

W.F. NORMAN COMPANY
P.O. Box 323
Nevada, MO 64772
417 667-5552 (in MO)
800 641-4038
metal ceilings

OLD FASHIONED THINGS
PLUMBING SUPPLY
402 S.W. Evangeline Thwy.
Lafayette, LA 70501
318 234-4800

OLD SOUTH COMPANY
P.O. Box 7096
Tarboro, NC 27886
919 823-8100
antique flooring

QUARRY CAST
Formglas Inc.
1015 Timothy Dr.
San Jose, CA 95133
408 283-1444
molded stone

THE RENOVATOR'S SUPPLY
6427 Renovator's Old Mill
Millers Falls, MA 01349
413 659-2241
plumbing and lighting
fixtures, hardware

ROY ELECTRIC CO. INC.
1054 Coney Island Ave.
Brooklyn, NY 11230
718 434-7002 (in NY)
800 366-3347
Victorian lighting fixtures

A. F. SCHWERD
MANUFACTURING
3215 McClure Ave.
Pittsburgh, PA 15212
412 766-6322
wood columns

SLEINMAN STUDIOS
423 Horsham Rd.
P.O. Box 527
Horsham, PA 19044
215 672-8404
restoration and custom-
made ornamental plaster

THE STEWART IRON
WORKS COMPANY
20 W. 18th St.
Covington, KY 41012-2612
606 431-1985

TREMONT NAIL CO.
P.O. Box 111
Wareham, MA 02571
508 295-0038
old-fashioned cut nails

URBAN ARCHAEOLOGY
285 Lafayette St.
New York, NY 10012
212 431-6969
authentic architectural
details salvaged from
buildings

VINTAGE WOOD WORKS
513 S. Adams
Box 1157
Fredericksburg, TX 78624
512 997-9513
solid wood Victorian
gingerbread detailing

VICTORIAN MILLWORKS
P.O. Box 2987
Durango, CO 81302
303 259-5915
wood moldings

J. P. WEAVER
2301 W. Victory Blvd.
Burbank, CA 91506
818 841-8462
decorative ornaments for
doors, mantles,
furniture, walls, ceilings

WORTHINGTON GROUP,
LTD.
P.O. Box 53101
Atlanta, GA 30355
404 872-1608
columns

BIBLIOGRAPHY

ART AND ARCHITECTURE BOOKS

Aldred, Cyril. *Egyptian Art in the Days of the Pharoahs 3100–320 B.C.* London: Thames and Hudson Co., 1980.

Arminjon, Catherine, et al. *L'Art de Vivre: Decorative Arts and Design in France 1789–1989.* New York: The Vendome Press, 1989.

Armstrong, Richard. *Artschwager, Richard.* New York: Whitney Museum of American Art, 1988.

Arnheim, Rudolf. *Art and Visual Perception.* Berkeley, Los Angeles, and London: University of California Press, 1974.

Barzini, Luigi. *The Italians.* New York: Atheneum, 1964.

Battersby, Martin. *Trompe L'Oeil.* New York: St. Martin's Press, 1974.

Bernheimer, Richard. *The Nature of Representation.* New York: New York University Press, 1961.

Borsook, Eve. *The Mural Painters of Tuscany from Cimabue to Andrea del Sarto.* Oxford: Clarendon Press, 1980.

Boutelle, Sara Holmes. *Julia Morgan, Architect.* New York: Abbeville Press, 1988.

Cardwell, Kenneth H. *Bernard Maybeck Artisan, Architect, Artist.* Santa Barbara and Salt Lake City: Peregrine Smith, Inc., 1977.

Cass, Caroline. *Modern Murals.* New York: Whitney Library of Design, 1988.

Filler, Martin. *Richard Haas Architectural Projects 1974–1988.* New York and Chicago: Brooke Alexander, Inc., and Rhona Hoffman Gallery, 1988.

Frankenstein, Alfred. *After the Hunt; William Harnett and Other American Still Life Painters.* Berkeley: University of California Press, 1969.

Gardner, Helen. *Gardner's Art Through the Ages.* 5th ed. Revised by Horst de la Croix and Richard G. Tansey. New York, Chicago, San Francisco, and Atlanta: Harcourt, Brace & World, Inc., 1970.

Garner, Philippe, ed. *The Encyclopedia of Decorative Arts 1890–1940.* New York: Van Nostrand Reinhold Company, 1978.

Geijer, Agnes. *A History of Textile Art.* London: Pasold Research Fund in Association with Sotheby Parke Bernet. 1976.

Goldberger, Paul, intro. *Richard Haas: An Architect of Illusion.* New York: Rizzoli, 1981.

Gombrich, E. H. *Art and Illusion.* Princeton, NJ: Bollingen Series XXV.5, Princeton University Press, 1960.

Grant, Michael. *The Art and Life of Pompeii and Herculaneum.* New York: Newsweek Books, 1979.

Janson, H. W. *History of Art.* Englewood Cliffs, NJ, and New York: Prentice-Hall, Inc., and Harry N. Abrams, Inc., 1967.

Jervis, Simon, intro. *Art & Design in Europe and America 1800–1900.* New York: E. P. Dutton, 1987.

Lee, Sherman. *A History of Far Eastern Art.* Englewood Cliffs, NJ, and New York: Prentice-Hall, Inc., and Harry N. Abrams, nd.

Mastai, M. L. d'Otrange. *Illusion in Art, Trompe l'Oeil: A History of Pictorial Illusionism.* New York: Abaris Books, 1975.

Matz, Friedrich. *The Art of Crete and Early Greece.* New York: Crown Publishers, Inc., 1962.

Milman, Miriam. *The Illusions of Reality: Trompe l'Oeil Painting.* Geneva and New York: Editions d'art Albert Skira and Rizzoli International Publications, Inc., 1982.

———. *Trompe-l'Oeil Painted Architecture.* Geneva and New York: Editions D'Art Albert Skira and Rizzoli International Publications, Inc., 1986.

Raeburn, Michael, ed. *Architecture of the Western World.* New York: Rizzoli International Publications Inc., 1980.

Ratcliffe, Carter. *Alex Katz Cutouts.* New York: Robert Miller Gallery, 1979.

Rybczynski, Witold. *Home: A Short History of an Idea.* New York: Penguin Books, 1986.

Shearman, John. *Mannerism.* Harmondsworth, England: Penguin Books Ltd., 1967.

van der Kemp, Gérald, Simone Hoog, and Daniel Meyer. *Versailles.* Trans. Bronia Fuchs. New York: Editions d'Art Lys, 1961.

DECORATING BOOKS

Busch, Akiko. *Wallworks.* Toronto, New York, London, Sydney, and Auckland: Bantam Books, 1988.

Dampierre, Florence de. *The Best of Painted Furniture.* New York: Rizzoli, 1987.

Entwisle, E. A. *The Book of Wallpaper.* London: Arthur Barker, 1954.

Facer, Nick. *Ornate Wallpapers.* New York: Harry N. Abrams, 1986.

Fleischmann, Melanie. *In the Neoclassic Style.* New York: Thames and Hudson, 1988.

Gilliatt, Mary. *Period Style.* London, England: Conrad Octopus Ltd., 1990.

Guild, Robin. *The Victorian House Book.* New York: Rizzoli, 1989.

Guild, Tricia and Elizabeth Wilhide. *Tricia Guild's Design and Detail: The Practical Guide to Styling a House.* New York: Simon and Schuster, 1988.

Krotz, Joanna L. *Metropolitan Home Renovation Style.* New York: Villard Books, 1988.

Miller, Martin and Judith. *Period Details: A Sourcebook for House Restoration.* New York: Crown Publishers, 1987.

———. *Period Design and Furnishing.* New York: Crown Publishers, 1989.

Nylander, Richard C. *Wallpapers for Historic Buildings.* Washington, D.C.: The Preservation Press, 1983.

———. *Wallpaper in New England.* Worcester, MA: Lavigne Press, 1986.

Praz, Mario. *An Illustrated History of Interior Decoration.* New York, Thames and Hudson Co., 1982.

Rense, Paige. *Architectural Digest Historic Interiors.* Los Angeles: Knapp Press, 1979.

Savage, George. *A Concise History of Interior Decoration.* New York: Grosset & Dunlap Publishers, 1966.

Thornton, Peter. *Authentic Decor.* New York: Viking Press, 1984.

Wissinger, Joanna. *Victorian Details.* New York: E.P. Dutton, 1990.

INSTRUCTION BOOKS

Bishop, Adele and Cile Lord. *The Art of Decorative Stenciling.* New York: Penguin Books, 1976.

Day, Joanne C. *The Complete Book of Stencilcraft.* New York: Dover Books, 1974.

Drucker, Mindy and Pierre Finklestein. *Recipes for Surfaces: Decorative Paint Finishes Made Simple.* New York: Simon & Schuster, 1990.

Fobel, Jim. *The Stencil Book.* New York: Holt, Rinehart & Winston, 1976.

Gottshall, Franklin H. *How to Design and Construct Period Furniture.* New York: Bonanza Books, 1989.

Hemming, Charles. *Paint Finishes.* Secaucus, NJ: Chartwell Books, 1985.

Innes, Jocasta. *Paintability.* London, England: Weidenfeld and Nicolson, 1986.

———. *Decorating with Paint.* New York: Harmony Books, 1986.

———. *Paint Magic.* New York: Francis Lincoln Publisher Ltd., 1989.

O'Neil, Isabel. *The Art of the Painted Finish.* New York: William Morrow, 1971.

Sloan, Annie. *Simple Painted Furniture.* New York: Weidenfeld and Nicolson, 1989.

Spencer, Stewart. *The Art of Marbling.* London, England: MacDonald & Co. Ltd., 1988.

Wilson, Althea. *Paint Works: The Art of Decorative Paint.* New York: Fawcett Columbine, 1989.

PERIODICAL ARTICLES

Barnett, Sheryl. "Reviving the Past." *Newsday Magazine,* Home Section, 24 September 1989, 54–56.

Blumenthal, Deborah. "They Can Fool Mother Nature." *Newsday Magazine,* Home Section, 24 September 1989, 62–63.

Costa, Robert. "Bidlo's Monstrous Eggs." *Arts Magazine,* vol. 62, no. 8, April 1988, 77.

Engardio, Pete, with Todd Vogel and Dinah Lee. "Companies Are Knocking Off The Knockoff Outfits." *Business Week,* 26 September 1988, 86.

Fairchild, John. "Chic Savages." *New York,* 16 October 1989.

Holley, Steven. "The Artful Dodger." *Home,* vol. 33, no. 8, August 1987, 52–57.

"In Paris, a Passion for Faux Chanel." *The New York Times,* 14 September 1988, C16.

Jacobs, Karrie. "Slaves to Fashion." *Metropolis,* vol. 7, no. 5, December 1987, 36–41, 57, 59, 61, 63.

Jacobson, Gianna. "Holy Bootlegger! What a Lot of Phony Batstuff!" *Business Week,* no. 3115, 17 July 1989, 70.

Kuspit, Donald. "Mike Bidlo, Leo Castelli." *Artforum,* May 1988, 141.

"No Copying." *The New York Times,* 5 November 1989, 7.

Sherman, Beth. "Playful Deceptions." *Newsday Magazine,* Home Section, 24 September 1989, 10–12, 14.

"Traditional Favorites." *House Beautiful,* vol. 131, no. 11, November 1989, 72–79.

Vogel, Carol. "High Point: New Reliables." *The New York Times Magazine,* 15 October 1989, 62.

Walker, Derek. "Architecture and Themeing." *Architectural Design,* nos. 9/10, June 1982, 28–32.

———. "Epcot 82." *Architectural Design,* nos. 9/10, June 1982, 2–5.

Ware, Mary Lee. "How Were The Glass Flowers Made?" *Botanical Museum Leaflets,* Cambridge, MA, Harvard University, vol. 19, no. 6, 9 January 1961.

Wechsler, Laurence. "Onward and Upward with the Arts (Value, Part II— Category Confusion)." *The New Yorker,* vol. 63, 25 January 1988, 88–98.

WuDunn, Sheryl. "What Lies Behind The Strange Smile on the 'Mona Lisa.'" *The New York Times,* 29 October 1989, H1, 41.

PHOTO CREDITS

courtesy of Baker Furniture, 177

Karen Becker, 170

courtesy of Christine Belfor Design Ltd., 116

Roger Benson, 72

© 1990 Andrew Bordwin for Paxwell Painting Studios, 76, 182

© 1989 Bob Braun, 52

courtesy of Braunstein/Quay Gallery, 66

courtesy of Brunschwig & Fils, 53, 97, 98, 99, 108, 109, 110, 112, 151, 163, 176

Steve Caspersen/Art Resource, NY, 202

© Tony Cenicola, 14, 67, 135

courtesy of Clarence House Fabrics Ltd., 103, 166, 185

courtesy of Colonial Williamsburg Foundation, 42, 141, 157

courtesy of Congoleum Corporation, 30, 114

Ali Elai, 204

© 1988 M. Elizabeth Ernst, 47, 119

© Paul Ferrino, 48

Gary Finkel, 56

courtesy of Fitz and Floyd, 15, 54, 127, 130

courtesy of F.B. Fogg, 120

courtesy of Formica Corporation, 43, 50

© The J. Paul Getty Museum, 33, 78

Oberto Gili for Ralph Lauren, 144

Joe Grant, 185 top

courtesy of Richard Haas Studio, 122

Francois Halard for Ralph Lauren, 10, 146

courtesy of Caryl Hall Studio, 161

© John Hall, 87, 101, 139, 143, 147, 159, 164, 165, 178

courtesy of OK Harris Works of Art, New York, 21, 60, 129

courtesy of Michael Harvey Ceramique, Inc., 128

Hawley Studio, 155

© Hearst San Simeon State Historic Monument/John Blades, 194, 195

courtesy of Heller Gallery, 58, 62, 63

courtesy of Henredon Furniture Industries, Inc., 57

Alan Herman, 184

Andy Holland, 179

Jason Hwang, 168

courtesy of International Fabrics, 185 bottom left

Kenro Izu, 197

© Peter Jordan, 192, 193

Tony King, 23

© Balthazar Korab, 188, 203

courtesy of Carlo Lamagna Gallery, 187

© Peter Margonelli, 7, 12, 26, 28, 29, 37, 40, 45, 46, 51, 61, 68, 69, 70, 71, 74, 75, 89, 90, 92, 113, 121, 126, 131, 132, 134, 136, 148, 150, 152, 153, 154, 158, 160, 171, 175, 180, 199, 200, 207

© Peter Mauss/ESTO, 107

The Metropolitan Musuem of Art, Rogers Fund, 1916, 156

The Metropolitan Museum of Art, Rogers Fund, 1939, 124

courtesy of Robert Miller Gallery, New York, 186 left

courtesy of Alexander F. Milliken Inc., 17, 208

© Michael Mundy, 81, 83

Mason Nye, 173

© Brian Oglesbee, 172

courtesy of Paxwell Painting Studios Inc., 20

Denes Petoe for Ralph Lauren, 11

Jill Pilaroscia, 198

© 1988 Jimmy M. Prybil, 6, 117, 174

© 1987 Bill Rothschild, 64, 86

© Curt Royston, 18, 19

Nicholas Sapieha/Art Resource, NY, 190

Scala/Art Resource NY, 22, 84

courtesy of Sculpture Placement, Ltd. of Washington DC; lifesize bronze sculptures by J. Seward Johnson, Jr., titled *The Winner*, 186 top right and *Sunday Morning*, 186 bottom right

courtesy of Shea & Beker Gallery Inc., 140

courtesy of F. Schumacher & Co., 94, 106

Steven Sloman/courtesy of Alexander F. Milliken Inc., 59

Steven Swieter, 36, 38, 39, 49, 85, 167, 169

courtesy of Christian Thee, 25, 73, 137, 181

© Michael Tropea, 105

Walter Uolde-Mariàm, 93, 111

© 1985 Brian Vanden Brink, 191

Rob Vinnedge, 32

© 1991 Paul Warchol, 8, 100, 104, 125

© Ellen Page Wilson, 77, 80, 96, 183

courtesy of Richard York Gallery, 34

INDEX